THE LAST

ALASKAN

MEXICAN

42 MOSTLY TRUE STORIES OF A FATHER AND SON IN THE LAST FRONTIER

CHARLES GONZALES

EALife

CONTENTS

This book is dedicated to my father, Papa Chuck.
To his soul, to his laughter,
to his good fortune and good luck.

This book is dedicated to the friends and family
who stuck with me along the way.
Y'all bring me back down to earth and remind me
to relax & breathe, er'y damn day.

This book is dedicated to the loved ones
I have held and lost.
You'll always be in my heart in Alaska,
Central Oregon, and San Antone,
like it or not.

Love y'all

ACKNOWLEDGEMENTS

First and foremost, there is one man I must thank above all else—Christ Jesus. He is the beginning, and the end. My Alpha, and my Omega. He helped pour these stories effortlessly from my soul, and he's still helping turn me into a writer (I've got a looooong way to go). I'm fairly certain he let the devil sit at my side during edits and proofreading though.

I have to thank my friends and family for encouraging me to write this crazy book. What began as a few short, social media posts have turned into one of the biggest, most fun projects of my life. The writing was easy, but the editing and vetting put more silver hairs on my head than I could ever imagine. That's why I am indebted to EABooks Publishing and their entire team who helped bring this book into the universe.

From Butch, the River Boat Captain on the Willow River, to the trumpeter who played Taps that gray afternoon in October on

Elmendorf Air Force Base, thank you for your service to my father. And to my three boys, Gabriel, Gavin, and Maxwell, I write this so you'll always have some memory of your grandfather, and I can't wait for you to read these stories for the first time...when you're old enough!

Lastly, to The Wisdom of Ben Sira, thank you for providing me the Old Testament, lessons of wisdom in these stories, some three thousand years later.

THANK YOU FOR YOUR CURIOSITY AND ENCOURAGEMENT

If you have this book in your hands right now, I want to thank you for taking the time to even consider picking it up to read. With the amount of options you have today to capture your attention, I consider your time and interest a great honor.

Maybe you picked it up because the title stood out to you. Maybe your intuition knew something was a little different when you saw the title. Perhaps you just needed a good laugh today and thought, "Mexicans in Alaska? What in the world is this about? A Mexican in Alaska? No way."

Right now you might be thinking . . .

"Is this an anthropology study?"

"Is this fiction?"

"Is this a comedy?"

"Is this about a father and his son?"

All will be answered in the following pages, but most importantly, I am very grateful that this book is in your hands. Thank you for helping bring this part of my life to fruition.

To my surprise, quite a few people eagerly responded as I wrote and posted some of these stories online about growing up in Alaska with my dad shortly after he passed away. So many people encouraged me to write a book because they actually enjoyed how I shared my stories (my English teachers are turning in their graves right now). What started as a way to help me process my father's passing turned into this book with 42 stories, and it's time for me to share these short stories of The Last Alaskan Mexican with the world.

Again, I want to emphasize that I'm not a writer by profession, and the most intelligent people I've ever met were English majors. I mean no disrespect to them by encroaching on their craft and livelihood, and if you're one of them, my writing style will drive you up a wall. You may want to keep the receipt for a refund. In fact, except for just one class at the University of Alaska, Fairbanks with professor D.A. Bartlette, I *loathed* all of my English and literature classes. And thank God for spell check and grammar-checking programs!

I *DO* promise to do my best to write from my soul, guided by my gut, while using a cool head and a warm heart to share these stories with you. FYI, I *never* take myself too seriously. Thank you for not taking me too seriously either.

Finally, this book is written in the spirit of one of my favorite books, *Wisdom Of Our Fathers*, by Tim Russert. It has a special place in my heart and is full of wonderful, short stories written by sons and daughters about their own fathers. These stories always make me smile and soften my heart quite a bit. I feel it's my time to help create a few new smiles and soften some hearts of sons and daughters throughout the world right now. I would encourage you to purchase his book for a wonderful Sunday morning read. Thank you, Mr. Russert. Please say hello to my father for me.

MY POWER OF WHY: TO BRING A SMILE AND A TEAR TO A MILLION FACES.

In his groundbreaking work on leadership, *Start With Why*, author Simon Sinek states, "People don't buy what you do, they buy why you do it." Why am I writing this book?

I was compelled to write this book about my own father to help me cope with his death (spoiler alert; sorry).

For me, sharing stories and making the world smile has always been part of my soul, especially with a sprinkle of BS for a few extra laughs. It makes me happy to make others laugh. When I think of writing stories to help me not be so damn angry at him for dying, I calm my mind and remember telling a story to my dad as we were sitting next to one of those Alaskan-sized campfires. I always loved his guttural and booming laugh, usually followed by a "Sheeeet-fire, LeRoy! You so full of dee shit, mister!" He yelled, in some kind of contrived, Alaskan-Mexican accent, with a touch of Texas Cowboy, followed by the smoker's cough for a minute. One of my favorite memories.

Smiles and tears: These are most important to me when writing this book for you to experience. Brining light to your day with a story, or even plucking at those tender heartstring to uncover and release those memories and emotions you forgot you remembered. I hope I've done that with this book.

This book's power of *WHY* unknowingly began on the morning of Sept 20th, 2022. My father's sister, my Aunt Vivian, called me early in the morning to deliver the news. I shiver anytime I see my father's number or one of his sibling's numbers on my caller ID, especially at my age. Usually, it means someone died, was in the hospital to prevent rapid unplanned disembarking, or was getting divorced.

I bet you get the same feeling when one of your parents calls you, right? "OMG. HOLY CRAP. OMG, Let begin rifling through the most horrific possibilities of what could have happened to someone in the family and prepare myself for the worst possible news," said every child born after Thomas Bell invented the telephone.

He was 76 and lived a life few Chicanos could even dream about. He made a career out of the Air Force, retired in The Great Land, built his home "25 miles from nowhere," as he would say, and spent his summers fishing for king, red, and silver salmon. He lived his life his own way, made his own rules, and reminded people about it every damn day. His personal theme song was "My Prerogative", and he never apologized for the way he lived his own life.

This book is for him. I owe it to him to do my best to preserve those epic stories so many have of him.

I try my best to *not* center my power of why around my own story when writing this book. Rather I try to focus the intention on my father, highlighting his jovial and stubborn nature to live his life the way he wanted, while simply taking me along for the ride. I've deleted many parts about my own childhood and experiences in order to bring you, the reader, closer to understanding my Baby Boomer father, rather than just writing about my own experiences growing up in Alaska. It's a difficult balance for me.

DIMMING MY OWN LIGHT

As I said, It's not my intention to write a memoir of my own struggles and success. While I grew up in the worst part of Anchorage in the 1970s and '80s, seeing things no child should be subjected to, this is a story about childhood, fatherhood, struggles, poverty, with lessons to take away from life. I don't harbor any resentment because of the circumstance which I was raised because it made me into the man and the father I am today. Besides, some of the ultra-bad decisions my family and I made ended up becoming some great stories (I guess the final book sales will determine if they're great stories or not), and all that matters now is sharing the memories of the experiences we had together. Am I still pissed that he died at the young age of 76? Of course, and I write more about that in chapter 32, but my gratitude is far greater than the weight of my anger.

I FORGOT I REMEMBERED SO MANY STORIES.

The more I wrote about one story, the more I remembered about another I had long forgotten. Like comedian Steven Write said, "Whenever I think about the past it brings back so many memories."

One story seemed to be the key to another and eventually, I unlocked 42 stories. I started keeping a list of words or phrases of each story, which later became the title chapters in this book. I wonder how many other stories I've already forgotten that I'll remember after this book is published? Maybe I'll write a Part II. The sequel is never as good as the original, though.

THE POWER OF WRITING

I'm sure that in some way, writing helps me navigate through the flood of emotions I've felt since he passed away. As a man, I am guilty of not talking and sharing too much about this process with my friends and family, but writing does help me constructively express the sorrow, joy, anger, and regret—all the things I experience in order for me to process this loss as I need to. I'm sure my father would appreciate that part of my learning/healing/coping process is to make other people laugh, chuckle, cry, and reminisce.

Men in particular are not great at communicating feelings; it's just not how we are wired. With a little practice, I've tried my best to communicate how I feel in these pages and connect with those who feel emotionally compromised because their father is no longer on the planet. I do believe losing a father is a right of passage, perhaps even a step into leadership and ambition. Losing my father does make me *not* want to half-ass things anymore and to use my whole ass now, instead.

For me, I feel what's very important when sharing these stories is that others (even some of his family members) might be able to learn, discern their own lessons, interpret their own meaning, and learn about the importance of forgiveness and reconciliation from these stories. At almost 50 years old, I'm still learning that part about being human.

In the Eskimo language, "Alaska" translates into "The Great Land." I think that means I need to become great at storytelling. It means I need to become great at many things like loving, forgiving, patience, parenting, leading, listening, and all the things online reels and shorts tell us we need to be. I'll do my best to be a good storyteller, as I work toward becoming a great one, one day. Remember, this is my first book, so please just wait at least a few days before you return it.

My father's death is a hard reminder that my time on this earth isn't eternal, and I shouldn't aim for "good" when it takes just a one percent more effort to aim for great. That's what The Great Land means to me. That's my own lesson I've learned from my father: Don't be afraid to lose. Don't be afraid to fail as you try to go from good to great.

For most people in the lower 48, Alaska is a gigantic, beautiful, mysterious place filled with snow, northern lights, and salmon the size of a third grade child. The state also boasts many amazing storytellers in tribes across the state. Maybe that's where I get some of my inspired writing from. I hope these big-fish-sized stories I thought I had forgotten will make your imagination run wild like the salmon on the Kenai River.

FYI, I'm sure other Alaskan-Mexicans are in the world (hell, the famous NHL player, Scotty Gomez went to high school just down the road from us). As such, I'm certain that neither my father nor I are actually The Last Alaskan Mexican. But I do believe that we carry the first and the last story within us to share with the world. I believe each of us has a unique library of experiences and lessons to offer. I believe sharing this part of my own Alaskan-Mexican library will hopefully bring some light-hearted happiness to your own world, somehow.

I hope this book inspires others to write something of their own or even to send me letters to share for the next book. I encourage you to immerse yourself in these stories and I hope they spark a few memories of your own stories you thought you had forgotten.

Plus, from what I've discovered, the simple answer to life is written in this book. IYKYK.

IS THIS BOOK FICTION OR NONFICTION?

Okay, sooo . . . this book is officially non-fiction but just like any good Alaskan book, I've included my own, big-fish stories. I'll leave the interpretations of each story up to you. The events are 99% true and I tell them in the most light-hearted way I know how. A little Taurus fertilizer helps produce beautiful roses—and at the end of the day, beautiful memories. Not all of these, mostly true stories are exclusively Alaskan or Mexican *per se*, but they all are simply about my father and me in Alaska.

NOTE: I will BS, but I won't lie. Bullshitting is just covering the truth with a blanket of fun that can be pulled off at any time and by anyone. Lying is attempting to bury the truth in the tundra, covering it up with dirt, snow, and ice (otherwise known as permafrost) so it can never be thawed out and exposed. I won't lie. I will often bullshit though.

WHO IS THIS BOOK FOR?

A mentor asked me why anyone would buy my book and who exactly I was writing it for. When my father died, I started sharing stories on social media just to put my thoughts into words, perhaps working through some kind of digital therapy, and maybe to connect with some of my friends and followers. As an author, I have to ask myself who I think will read this book, and more importantly, why they should buy it.

If you're a Gen-Xer like me, or maybe an early-model Millennial, this book is for you because our parents are expiring, and I believe our stories about them should be shared with our sons and daughters, and their own sons and daughters.

If you're a Boomer like my father, it means you're from his generation, and you understand him in ways I never will. Yes, this book is for you too, Boomer, and it means a hell of a lot to me that it's in your hands right now (or on your tablet).

If you have a dad, this book is for you.

If you are a child of alcoholic parents, this book is for you.

If you are a dad, this book is for you.

If you've lost a dad, this book is for you.

If you need to smile every once in a while, and want to remember some stories about your own dad, this book is for you.

If you're from Alaska, this book is *definitely* for you.

If you've ever been angry at your father, this book is for you.

If you're scared of losing your dad, and you want to remember some things you've forgotten about him, this book is written for you.

Thousands of these fathers, these heroes, are expiring every day. They are part of a generation that fought for their country when it mattered. Many of them fought for their families, shaped a country with wrenches and WD-40, and had eyes the color of exhaustion. Libraries could be filled with stories of these men, and I believe we, as their children, have a duty to share some of those stories with the world before all of these memories are lost to the ages.

A BRIEF HISTORY OF THE LAST ALASKAN MEXICANS

"Mexicans" and "Alaska" generally are not nouns that co-exist in the same sentence. There is an irony, perhaps even comedy in exploring the intersection of these two, polar opposite cultures (yes, we make snowmariachis instead of snowmen).

In my 48 years, the subject is still a conversation catalyst:

"Wait, you're a Mexican from Alaska? Does that make you Meximo?"

"Mexican Alaskan? The mukluk Mexican?"

"Ooooh, is that why you're so white?"

"Mexican Alaskan? The Icespic?" is my all-time favorite. Scheduled to be trademarked, too.

I've heard them all . . . which in fact are *not* very many, but they still make me laugh. Like I said, I never take myself too seriously.

We (Hispanics/Chicano/Latinos/Mexicans/

Mexican-Americans/LatinX—whatever we are referred to these days) are not exactly indigenous to the northern land of ice and snow, so I understand how this book seems a little out of the ordinary.

Some people hypothesize that the Chinese people populated Mexico and all of North America when they migrated across the Russian-Alaskan land bridge centuries ago. Since then, our Mexican blood cells have thawed out, and we just exist better near agave and cactus plants than we do near glaciers and flying reindeer.

Ironically, Alaska was discovered by a British explorer named Captain James Cook, but the tides were so fast and it was so damn cold that he "turned" his ship around ASAP to get back to the warmer islands of the South Pacific, where the natives subsequently tied him to a stake, lit him on fire, and ate him after they realized he was not, in fact, a god (true story). I feel this same thing would happen to me if I moved to Mexico.

To this day two bodies of water and a mountain range in Alaska— are named after the doomed captain: 1) Cook Inlet; 2) Turnagain Arm, and; 3) The Medium-Rare Mountain Range. Too soon? Okay, the first two are true, anyway.

I was one of a handful of military babies born and raised in the '70s in Anchorage, Alaskan. If a Mexican is born in Alaska, his or her dad or mom is in the Army or Air Force. Chicanos in Alaska are all military brats because their parents were given their Alaskan installation orders for three to four years. After their tour is completed, many times the parents fall in love with the solitude, the beauty, the zero income tax and the money they pay you to live there, so they choose to stay there and call it their home (that is what my dad did).

Yes, Alaska is beautiful, but it's a very isolated place with either perpetual darkness or continual sunshine. With either ten feet of snow and ice or swarms of vampire mosquitos trying to kill you. With exorbitantly high-priced blueberries and groceries, but the best tap water in the country (especially in Girdwood).

Yes, it's a stunning place that everyone should visit at least once in his or her lifetime, but it's sort of like Las Vegas—just go for a vacation and don't live there (I also lived in Vegas for two years).

The people who live there are the very best part of Alaska. They stick tightly together in their tribes and inner circles, ironically because of their isolation from the lower 48 and the rest of civilization. Their separation from the mainland creates a certain sense of "social rogue-independence" among the people, which outsiders wouldn't understand. I'll explain what an "outsider" is later.

This can make many Alaskans incredibly stubborn and independent. One of those hard-headed, stubborn, rogue Sourdoughs was my father—a Los Angeles-born, five-foot-ten-inch, hood-rat Cholo, who joined the Air Force and made a life worth telling a story about in The Great Land. Don't worry, I have a glossary of terms at the end of this book, explaining Alaskan terminology.

ORIGINS

My dad wasn't Alaskan. Carlos, or "Chuck" as he was known to his friends, "Charlie" to his family, was born in East Los Angeles and grew up in an area called Echo Park. He was one of ten baby-boomer-generation kids of the Gonzales/Gomez family tree. His dad, Polo *Gonzalez* was a cotton picker from Brownsville, Texas, then an entrepreneurial, television repairman who moved to Los Angeles.

Polo became the first *Gonzales** small business owner when he opened his own TV shop, Gonzales & Sons, where he taught his sons about electronics. This led my father, the oldest of the Gonzales clan, to join the U.S. Air Force, where he became an aircraft electrician on fighter planes. After he enlisted, he received his orders for Alaska, and he decided to spend nearly 50 years there when his tour was over.

He lived his final days in the beautiful Last Frontier, from the comfort of his couch—with an Alaskan-sized view from his living room that most of us could only dream about.

Technically I'm a Mexican-Alaskan-American who doesn't speak Spanish none-too-good, with grandparents from Texas, Colorado, Mexico City, and Aguacalientes. I was born and raised Alaskan, but you can't call me a native Alaskan. In Alaska, if you're Native Alaskan, you're an indigenous person and belong to an official tribe like Eskimo, Tkinket, Athabaskan, or the long-forgotten Seahawk tribe.

Yes, the elusive Seahawk tribe of Alaska is a group of less than 500,000, who were forced to accept their northern obligation from birth to cheer for the closest geographical NFL team. To this day, the Seahawks are known as "Alaska's Team." I had to leave ASAFP in 2000 because I'm a diehard Rams fan, thanks to Dad.

Dad always had the type of personality to make everyone laugh and make sure everyone was having a good time. And damn, was he loud. Were all Baby Boomers that loud on Sunday afternoons when watching their favorite football team? Dad was always the loudest to cheer for the Rams anytime we went out to a restaurant or bar to watch them play, every other weekend on a Sunday.

He picked up the goofy gene from somewhere, and for the life of me, I can't figure out where he found it. I might have a sliver of his goofy gene, but his was definitely was next-level goofy. I still smile when I think about his laughter, and if it weren't for his goofy gene, I wouldn't have these stories to write.

In 1999, he moved to Knik, Alaska with his wife, Wilma, and he *loved* living in the middle of nowhere, where no one would bother him, where traffic didn't get in his way, where he wasn't forced to make small talk, and where he could pee off his own deck while having a smoke and shooting a 9mm out into the tundra (that's a big deal in Alaska).

But no matter how far he strayed away from Echo Park in East L.A., he never forgot about his heritage, and he tried to make sure I knew who I was and where my roots came from.

I'm sure most of Gen Xers' parents are incredibly proud of their heritage. Even though my dad was a bit out of place, he still loved menudo, Santana, lowriders, very sad songs about women breaking men's hearts, and all things Mexicano. But it's difficult to preserve that culture when a person lives so far out of his or her element. Sure, he tried to make enchiladas with me, but it was with the cheapest can of green sauce from the grocery store, with chilis that were a month old and wilted, because very few fresh veggies exist in Alaska when everything has to be shipped in from outside.

Without being too stereotypical, he did drive a Monte Carlo lowrider with gold rims, and he loved his American pilsner beer with the logo of a little Mexican senorita sitting on the moon. That's what he told me, anyway.

No, you can't call me a Native Alaskan. Instead, you can call me The Icespic (I coined that term first). People not from Alaska are called *outsiders*, and even the lower 48 is referred to as "outside." Outsiders ask me two questions when I tell them I'm from Alaska. From my experience, this is a universal law, similar to Newton's Third Law of Motion: Action and Reaction:

Laws Of Questions To a Mexican From Alaska:

Q1. How in the hell did a Mexican end up in Alaska?

Q2. What do you miss about Alaska?

I'll get into the details and answers in my 42 short stories.

ORDER OF STORIES

These stories are mostly in chronological order, starting in about 1980, as those are my earliest memories, through 2022.

MY OWN LESSONS

Each story is followed by a lesson that I've done my best to interpret, with the help of a little Wisdom. They are certainly not the only lessons, they're just ones that resonated with me. I'd love to hear what unique lessons you gather from these stories.

If you take away one thing from this book, let it be this: 1) Don't ever take yourself too seriously, and 2) WD-40 stands for "Water Displacement–Number 40." It took the Army 40 tries to get it right. My dad was in the Air Force and could have done it in ten. #TrueStory #WD-10

SHARE YOUR OWN STORIES ABOUT YOUR FATHER

I would absolutely be honored to read your own story about the man you call your father. Please email your story to: chuck@ TheLastAlaskanMexican.com

DON'T BLOCK THE EMOTIONS

If you become emotional reading this book, don't block the flow. Let it out as hard as you need. Known as "emoting," I'd encourage you to marinate in the happiness, the sorrow, or the anger from any memories of your own time with your father. You don't have to stand guard at the gate of your pain, but instead simply open the gates and allow it to safely flow out of you. "Emote" those emotions and envelop yourself in your own humanity. I know it is difficult for most men to emote, so whether you need to be alone or with someone you trust for support, open the door to that which is buried deepest within you.

A SPECIAL REQUEST TO ALCOHOLICS

If you are an alcoholic or the child of alcoholic parents, there is certainly no romanticizing the effects uncontrollable alcoholism. In these stories, in telling these stories, I try to find the silver lining around the cloud. It's not fun, it's not optimistic, and it's not enjoyable for a kid to experience. Watching loved ones destroy their lives with alcohol isn't a boastful claim to maturity. It's a thief of joy, an inhibitor of education, a bandit of optimism. My reconteur in life and in this manuscript is just one way I deal with the events of my childhood. I have to encourage any child of an alcoholic parent to find a way to deal with that kind of pain and suffering. And, if you're an alcoholic parent of a child, please don't wait another day to get help, and don't lose hope. The irretrievable moments you're not remembering with your children are are lost for you, but the alcoholic-vicissitude become seared into long-term memories for them. It's never too late and it doesn't matter how old you are, you can always start the journey of sobriety and make the most out of the remaining heartbeats and moments you have with the people who love you the most. For the love of your children, maybe even to repair the damage inflicted on your relationship with them, please seek the humility and forgiveness Christ has to offer, because he is our strength (Isaiah 41:10). Know that being humble, offering apologies, and seeking forgiveness are never weaknesses. They're superpowers.

Alcohol is the weakness. The devil is weakness. It's never too late.

—Charles Gonzales, a proud son

CHAPTER 1

THE MEXICAN JUMPING BEAN

One of the earliest memories I have of my dad involves booze and acro-batics. Most of my memories about my dad involve booze, but that's what makes them so funny and memorable for me. Dad was what some would call, "a happy drunk."

My parents and I lived in the nastiest, crumpled-beer-can, ghetto, single-wide trailer, on the muddiest dirt road in Anchorage, in an area called Spenard (I cannot for the life of me figure out why or how the trailer park is still standing today, more than 50 years later). One night, when I was about six years old, and after a bit of drinky-drinky by both my mom and dad, I bet my dad he could not copycat everything I did. I was young, so I was still nimble and thought my father was too.

"Okay Dad, you have to try to copy everything I do! Ready? Okay, spin around, like this!" And he spun around as best as a grown, intoxi-cated man could spin.

"Okay Dad, run in place, like this!" And he ran in place.

"Okay, jumping jacks, like this!" And he did ten gangly and intoxicated jumping jacks as best as he could.

Then, I stood on our wooden coffee table. Bad idea (for dad, anyway).

"Dad, stand on top of the coffee table, jump in the air, spin around, and land on your feet, like this! You can do it!"

And he stood on top of the coffee table, looking like a bigass, Mexican luchador (a luchador is a Mexican wrester) with his hands on his hips. He jumped as high as our seven-foot, asbestos-tile ceiling would let him, spun around, and I swear he belted out, "Ariba! Ariba!"

All 220 pounds of him crashed down *through* the floor! *Boom!* Smack dab, on his ass *and straight* through the carpet and particleboard subfloor, right down onto the dirt below the trailer!

My God, if he were only wearing a luchador mask, that would have been stereotypically perfect!

"Chuck! What in the hell did you do!" My mom screamed at him.

I still remember standing on what was left of the living room floor, looking down at him, holding my belly with both hands and laughing hysterically. I can still see him clearly in my mind, sitting on the dirt, but what stood out most to me the most were all the utility lines under the trailer, which I thought looked so weird. He just sat there, smushed between the gas, water, and electric lines, with a dazed look on his face that said, "What in the hell just happened to me, and how much will this cost to fix?"

I just kept laughing. Here I am, 48 years old, and I'm still laughing.

How did he fix it? He bought a piece of plywood, slid it under the carpet, and we all walked over and looked at that damn bulge for the next eight years. An unconscious step, but a memory at each passing of what had happened in that spot (the trailer is still standing, and I wonder if that bulge is still there).

That's when I realized I had a goofy dad, whom I'd probably have a good time with in the years to come. And did we ever.

LESSON:

Whiskey can drown the crown of wisdom one earns in their life, and while bad decisions make for great stories, listening to your inner voice of contemplative thought and reason can save hundreds of dollars in mobile home, subfloor repairs, and heating bills in the winter. Don't downplay that voice, ever.

CHAPTER 2

THE MOUTH
OF THE WILLOW

M y dad always took me fishing during the Alaskan summers. I was nine years old in 1983, when we drove up the Alaskan Highway to a little town called Willow, to see who could land the biggest king salmon of the season.

Sometimes we'd leave after he got off work on Friday nights, close to midnight, because he always worked the swing shift on Elmendorf Air Force Base in Anchorage. I was so excited I could *never* sleep while I waited for him to pick me up from my mom's trailer, because my old man was taking me camping and fishing in Alaska.

I'd peek out the window to watch for his headlights. Nothing. I'd peek again. Nothing. I'd peek again and, *yes!* I saw the headlights of his Monte Carlo! He was finally here!

After a two-hour drive up north, we'd spend the night sleeping in our car, in a dirt parking lot, in front of a rustic Alaskan bar just off the highway. He wanted us to be the first ones to charter a boat with Captain Butch the next morning so we could snag a great camping spot and fishing hole. Most great fishing holes in Alaska require either a two-hour drive, a float plane, or an airboat to get to.

Captain Butch was everything you'd think an Alaskan river guide would be. A 60-plus-year-old, scraggly-bearded man wearing a baseball cap on top of his unbrushed, shoulder-length silver mane, covered head-to-toe in brown, outdoor gear, hip waders, a perpetual cigarette in his mouth, and nicotine stains on the sides of his mustache. He captained a flat-bottom, aluminum-weld boat to take people upstream on the river, dropping us off at the prime fishing spot where the kings waited for us, at the mouth of the Willow.

We'd load up the boat and slice upstream through the river, dodging polar bears, porcupines, wolves, massive floating logs, rapids, beluga whales, and icebergs along the way. Finally, we landed at "The Mouth" to unload our gear and a couple cases of his beer.

We'd pitch the tent, strung up the Ugly Stick fishing poles with Spin-N-Glos and fish eggs we'd cured from the previous season, and walk to the banks of the Willow to find a spot to start combat fishing.

Combat fishing is shoulder-to-shoulder fishing, with anglers' lines *constantly* getting tangled. If you were lucky, you had a boat anchored to the shore and then fished out of the back of it to avoid all of the other fishermen's lines. Someone saw me, a lonely kid on the shore fishing, and they invited me into their boat. *Score!*

After a few hours of fishing, Dad decided to walk back to camp for a bite to eat. I stayed on the river fishing because I was in the groove, and I was near a sweet-spot fishing hole, where I knew the kings hung out. Not 30 seconds after he left, I felt a tug on my line. After I felt a second tug, I knew I had hooked a monster. I almost yelled, "DAD! DAD! I'VE GOT ONE!" But at nine years old, fishing next to a bunch of salty men and women on the river, no way was I going to scream out for my daddy to help me.

"Keep your tip up!" all the adults screamed at me. "Reel it in!" they yelled. "Keep your tip up!"

When you hook into a king salmon, it feels like you're playing tug-o-war with a nine hundred pound gorilla. At nine years old, I thought I was fighting Moby Dick, and I couldn't wait to land it and show it off!

I fought as hard as I could trying to keep the tip of my Ugly Stick up. Reeling and pulling, reeling and pulling. I thought for sure it would drag me over into the drink.

Finally, after what seemed like an eternity, I landed my first king salmon and enjoyed a huge round of applause from the grown-ups. Damn, I was one happy boy! I dragged it up the bank, then all the way back to camp, through the dirt, to where I found my dad, standing by the fire in his rain gear, with a Tareyton cigarette hanging out of his mouth and beer in hand.

"What the heck! Why didn't you yell for me? I missed you catching your first fish!"

"Um, there was no way I was screaming for my daddy when I hooked this thing. No way, sorry, Dad."

"Ha, ha, ha! You didn't want to seem like a big baby, crying for his daddy? Well, shitfire, LeRoy, you did it!"

Forty-two inches, thirty-eight pounds of king salmon fish. You never forget your first.

After that, I laid down for a nap, since I was super tired after staying up, waiting for him earlier that night. Most of the time, whenever I woke up and climbed out of the tent, I'd find a king salmon bigger than the one I caught, laying next to mine, gutted, and stuffed with grass (to keep it from drying out), and there was dad, sitting by the fire, looking at me with a smile on his face.

That is, until Wilma, the woman who would later become my stepmother, started coming with us and *always* had the last laugh as she laid her trophy king salmon next to our little, humble minnows. That's one woman I could never out-fish.

Come Sunday afternoon, when it was time to pack it up and head home, Butch would arrive to pick us up in his flat-bottom, aluma weld, Alaskan river boat:

Butch would say, "Hey Chuck, how did you do this weekend? Did you get smoked again by your wife and kid?"

Dad responded, "Shut up and just take my money again, Butch."

Back to Anchorage, we went.

A few years later, dad realized he was sitting on an Alaskan gold mine. In true Latino style, Dad refused to let *any* of that fish go to waste. After we gutted it at the river and packaged the meat in cans, he put the carcass on ice in the cooler for the trip home. Dad would bury the salmon carcass in a pile of topsoil he'd save for the following summer, making his own Alaskan black gold soil to use for his rose garden. Yep, Dad had a Latino green thumb after all.

The fact is, I couldn't even stand the taste of salmon when I was a kid. I gave all my fish to my dad so he could can them up and ship a case down to our family in LA. They loved eating it, and I loved catching it with my dad. Oh, if they ever knew the stories behind that succulent king and red salmon!

LESSON:

With our fishing poles in hand, his beers and a pack of cigarettes tucked away in the oversized pocket of his green, government-issued rain jacket, we found peace sitting on the banks of the mouth of the Willow in Alaska. Beneath those birch and spruce trees, no one and nothing could make us afraid, ever. Was it the fish we went for each year? Never. I never went fishing with my dad just for the fish.

CHAPTER 3

THE BEAR ON THE RUSSIAN

My dad loved exploring Alaska, especially driving a country mile to find the best fishing holes for kings, silvers, or reds.

One weekend when I was little, umm, I mean, when I was younger (yeah, I'm five-foot-eight-and-a-quarter-inch on a good day), Dad drove our family down to the Russian River campground in South Central Alaska. Located about two hours south of Anchorage, the Russian River campground is a beautifully scenic, Alaskan campground, nestled in a forest of black spruce trees and sliced by icy, turquoise rivers. The silt from the glaciers that is washed out into the rivers absorbs shorter wave length light, such as purple and indigo. The green and blues are scattered back to our eyes, which create the most beautiful rivers you'll ever see. Now, they're just blue reflections in my memory here in San Antonio.

The strength of the current is what makes the salmon so big and strong as they migrate upstream to spawn. The freezing-cold water must make the salmon extra angry, which is why they put up such a fight when you hook into one. Black and brown bears flock to the area to take advantage of the all you can buffet of angry, muscular salmon, and also campground side-dish goodies.

Sometime around 1981, and over the 4th of July weekend, Dad drove my mom, my sister, and me to the campsite in the same car made famous by Wayne and Garth; the 1970s, brown and stunningly beautiful (wink, wink), AMC Pacer. Yep, a Pacer. It may not have been the prettiest, but what I wouldn't give to ride shotgun with him just one more time in that thing.

When we arrived at our campsite, I remember helping Dad set up camp and string up the tent. It was the old, six-man, green Army tent that needed a rope attached to every tree in the damn forest to keep it from blowing down. It did have a cool, little, collapsible window, though.

After what seemed like a few hours of tying the tent to trees then fishing on the Russian River, we all went to sleep in the tent. But something woke my mother; a noise from outside in our campsite. She looked out the little zip-up window and saw a black bear rummaging around our campsite.

In a loud whisper, she yelled, Kids! Wake up and get to the car There's a bear outside!"

"What? Mom, why are we going outside when there's a bear out there?" I said.

"Don't argue with me! Just do what I say!' She said. (IDK about your mom, but mine said that *a lot!*)

Black bears that live close to the rivers in south central Alaska are bigger than inland black bears because of the supply of fish and calories to fatten them up. In other words, we had a *big* black bear problem on our hands.

We carefully unzipped the door to the tent, quietly snuck out, and tip-toed to the Pacer. We sat there in the car, peering through the windshield. I was terrified, and my heart was pounding out of my chest. But *my dad stayed in the tent!* Crazy Chicano!

The bear continued to wander around our campsite and I specifically remember it stealing the cauliflower we had wrapped in aluminum foil sitting on top of our cooler. The bear left the campsite, realized how shitty-tasting raw cauliflower is, then came back to the campsite to see what else he could get his claws on to satisfy his Alaskan-sized appetite. My dad had a plan though. Not a great plan, but he had a plan.

He brought along one of those, long, aluminum, metal tubes that attached as a handle to household vacuums from the '70s. Why did he bring it on a camping trip? To shoot bottle rockets out on the 4th of July, of course! The goofy gene.

IDK what it is about Mexicans and fireworks. I mean, leave it to this vato to bring fireworks in the middle of the Alaskan forest, where there's only a two-lane road in *and* out of the place, and a million tourists that time of year. Seriously, Dios mio, *Santa Maria*, Papa!

This guy stayed in the tent, lit the bottle rockets, shoved them into the tube, pointed it out of the window straight at the thieving black bear, and *boom!* He shot that black bear right in the butt with the bottle rockets!

The bear took off yelping down the hill as fast as he could and never came back. My mom, sister, and I spent the rest of the night in the Pacer, Dad stayed in the tent, armed with his homemade, bear-defense-system to keep his family and vegetables safe.

I don't remember catching any fish that weekend, but I think I finally understand why I really don't like cauliflower all that much. As I said on the Willow, going fishing isn't just about going fishing.

Good thinking, Dad.

LESSON:

A timid heart will seek few adventures. But a heart of courage and a few bottle rockets can save your family from a hungry, pesco-vegetarian black bear.

CHAPTER 4

BAPTIZED ON OLVERA STREET IN LOS ANGELES

*D*ad was baptized Catholic on the streets in Los Angeles. He had nine brothers and sisters: Richard, Bobby (every large Mexican family in L.A. at the time had a Richard and Bobby), Gilbert, Danny, Ruben, Sally, Mary, Vivian, and Yolanda. As far as I know, they were all baptized on the oldest street in Los Angeles—Olvera Street.

But, I was born in Alaska not L.A., so I didn't get the privilege of being sprinkled with holy water on Olvera Street Sunday morning, right before the Rams played.

I was born at Providence Hospital in Anchorage to unwed, CEO, Catholic parents. What's a CEO Catholic? Christmas and Easter Only. Other than that, we never, never attended Sunday Mass.

After I was born, my dad went to the local parish near our trailer park to talk with the priest about having me baptized.

"Hey, Father, I'd like to have my kid baptized."

"Okay Mr. Gonzales, sure we can do that. Are you a practicing Catholic?"

"Not really."

Thinking for a second, he asked my father, "Okay, maybe we can work on that? Are you a member of our parish?"

"Nope, " Dad said. Trying to find something to stick to the wall, the priest asked, "Okay, do you regularly go to Mass?"

"No man, football is on Sunday, and you know, they're usually tape-delayed games."

"Well, do you have godparents chosen for the boy?"

"No, Father," said my dad.

"Well, Mr. Gonzales, we need to make sure that the boy will be raised Catholic in accordance with scripture and we'd like you to learn how we recommend the catechism should be lived by the family."

"Father, the boy's mom and I aren't married yet. We're just living together."

"What the shit, over . . . " (okay, the priest didn't use one of my dad's catch phrases I'll explain those in a few chapters, but you get the idea)."Mr. Gonzales, we still need you and his mother to attend an informational meeting on raising children Catholic and following the catechism of the church."

"Wait a minute, man. I could go down to Olvera Street in L.A. and get him baptized in an hour," my dad replied."Well, Mr. Gonzales, we do things a little differently these days since Vatican II, and. . . . "Piss on this horseshit!" My dad yelled.

If you ever knew my dad, you know those were the exact words that frequently came out of his mouth. After that day, after talking with that priest, he never, never went back to Mass again on Christmas *or* Easter! He was just a N.A.C. "Never Again Catholic"—and he was never one to flee from sin and fun. He wasn't even a Taurus, but damn, he was the most stubborn man I've *ever* known.

He never had me baptized and instead just gave me the decision on how to handle my own spiritual salvation. He didn't want to deal with the administrative process of having his children enter the kingdom of God.

He did enroll me in Catholic school for a few years. He knew private school was best for me, and he was willing to make the sacrifice to get me there during those years. But he always left the decision up to me.

I visited Dad in 2019, and surprisingly, I actually got him to step into a parish to go to Mass for the first time in 40 years. As luck would have it, it was a poorly conducted Mass, and when it was over, I think he was even happier that he chose to spend his Sundays watching football all those years.

Olvera Street is a really cool place in downtown L.A. , and if you have the opportunity, head down there to just relax in a cool cantina, spot a few celebs (we ran into Nick Cage down there and got a picture with him), and watch a few Latino babies get baptized across the street on Sunday before the Rams play.

I went down there while on vacation a few years ago just to see the church where my dad was baptized. It was overflowing with Mexicanos preparing food for the homeless and those in need. It made my heart full to see that kind of generosity.

When my family in Los Angeles found out I went to Olvera Street at night by myself, well, they weren't very happy.

"Charles, what are you doing, and where have you been? You're too white to be down there! It's not safe for you! Get your ass back here to Covina!"

LESSON:

In words and in deeds, if we are willing, we honor a father because a good dad does his best, and kindness to him won't be forgotten. Fathers may not be perfect, and maybe they don't attend Mass each Sunday, but our R-E-S-P-E-C-T for our fathers is like a get-out-of-jail-free card, and one day it will be like warmth over Alaskan tundra, melting away even our own worst mistakes.

CHAPTER 5

POPE JOHN PAUL II VISITS ALASKA

A s I am writing this, it happens to be *The Feast of St. John Paul II* in the Catholic Church. *My dad was a cradle Catholic, and he actually took me to see Pope John Paul II when he came to Anchorage, on February 22, 1981. I was six years old, and I can't believe I still remember this story. It has to be one of my oldest memories of my dad and me together.*

We all still lived in the trailer in 1981, which was about five to six miles from where the Pope was hosting an outdoor Mass and giving people his blessing at The Park Strip. Dad and I walked the whole way together—probably because he just didn't want to pay for parking. LOL!

This was in February in Alaska, the dead of winter, but I don't remember it being cold at all. I just remember walking and camping with my dad. I can only imagine why my Father wanted to walk with his six-year old son on sidewalks, trails and through the

Alaskan woods to see Pope John Paul: For the pursuit of another experience, which he was never too afraid to take.

I've heard that no one in history has been seen by more people in person than PJPII. I find that hard to believe, because in 2023, The Rolling Stones recently released what seems like their *one millionth* album and were still touring. Surely more people have seen the Stones than the PJPII.

I can still remember Dad in his green military jacket and freighter frame backpack (I can't believe I remember the name of that thing). We had left the house the afternoon before the Pope arrived, and strapped to the backpack were a tent and sleeping bags. Along with about 100 other tent campers, we picked a spot on the grass to call our home for the night. It was so fun for a six-year-old, and I don't even remember complaining along the way.

Dad had packed raw hot dogs, canned beans, and water. I'm pretty sure a flask of whisky was also stowed away in there somewhere. Though we didn't have a fire, I was content camping in the middle of Anchorage with my dad for the night, just to see one of the most famous men in the world, who I had absolutely no clue about. For me, it wasn't about the Pope. It was just about camping with my dad and eating hot dogs wrapped in white bread.

Morning came, and I popped my head with my big ol' fro out from the tent to see people starting to arrive. More and more people packed the open field, and Dad wanted a to be sure we got a good spot to watch Mass.

The Park Strip is just a long stretch of grassy area, so when 10,000 people showed up, it turned into a gigantic mud pit . . . in the winter. Dad brought his bunny boots with him just for this reason. What are bunny boots, you ask? They're gigantic, white rubber boots that winter soldiers and snow ninjas wear, and excellent for keeping your feet warm during the long Alaskan winters.

Before we began our muddy trek toward the stage to get a good view of the Holy See, Dad turned to me and asked, "You need to use the bathroom, kid?" There was a long row of honey buckets lined along the side of the Park Strip.

"No, I'm okay, Daddy." I hated those things, and I always thought something would rise up out of the bog of eternal feces and pull me in. Dad called it, *"Attack of the shit monster!"* Lol!

"Okay, kid. Because once we get up there, you won't be able to come back and use it."

"No, Daddy, I don't have to go. I'll be okay."

I heard the crowd beginning to roar in the distance. Far off, I could see the Popemobile driving toward us, with PJPII waving to everyone. He looked so small.

Dad and I stood in the mud-soaked field with everyone else and watched the Pope take the stage.

"In nomine Patris et Filii et Spirits Sancti." The Pope said with his thick, Polish accent.

Five minutes later, guess who had to go pee? Yep, this kid.

Dad was not happy. I still remember that look on his face, but this time he didn't yell one of his popular catchphrases he was obviously thinking (I'm guessing it was, "Oh my achin' ass.") Instead, with a super-annoyed look on his face, he said, "Excuse me. Excuse me, sir. Excuse me, ma'am, my kid has to use the potty. Excuse me."

We stood in line with a lot of other people in front of those green outhouses of death, and even though I was at a Mass delivered by the Pope, watched over by an army of holy angels, I was sure I would be pulled into the depths of hades by the poop demon.

Although I avoided a near-death experience, we couldn't get back to the spot we had near the stage. There were just too many people to navigate through. We watched the Pope from the distance of our tent near the honey buckers. We *did* get our blessing though—not by him, but by one of the eucharistic ministers on the stage, which I was kind of bummed about.

We packed it up after Mass and began the journey home. It was our very own adventure, albeit an *expected journey* (that joke is for J.R.R. Tolkien geeks!). Since then I always thought it was such an honor that the Pope chose to visit little Anchorage, taking time out of his schedule to see our tiny city, on our little, muddy Park Strip.

The Pope was shot three months later in Rome on May 13th, 1981, just one day before my seventh birthday, and from then on, he rode in the glass-encased "Popemobile"—like the Batmobile, but with plexiglass instead of rocket boosters.

Pope John Paul died on April 5th, 2005. Dad died on September 20th, 2022. I hope they're both sitting in heaven right now, looking down at where we all were in Anchorage, laughing . . . wishing they would have scheduled his Alaskan visit in July or August instead.

LESSON:

With your whole heart honor your father and respect the journeys he takes you on, for when you do, you'll have a wonderful experience to share with your own children one day, and the evil poop monsters will not overtake you!

*Search this on Google images and you will see the line of honey buckets on the edge of the Park Strip.

CHAPTER 6

CHUNKY MONKEY IN THE F-15

D*ad was an electrician on fighter planes when he joined the U.S. Air Force. Not too many kids get the chance to sit in the cockpit of a U.S. Air Force, F-15 Eagle, but I was one of the lucky ones. Calvin and his stuffed tiger would be proud.*

Dad worked on F-15 Eagles, F-16 Fighting Falcons, F-4 Phantoms, and anything else the Air Force told him to fix. The F-15 was always my favorite.

He worked in a big hangar called "The Alaskan Eagle Keeper" on Elmendorf AFB in Anchorage, and I always loved walking through the doors to that shop. On some of our weekends together after the divorce, he'd have a bit of work to do on base, and I would get to spend a few hours with him in the electric shop. I'd see the airmen working at their MS-DOS computer terminals, or some just striding around, shuffling through a stack of papers in their hands.

Then, they would disappear behind the bay doors into the Eagle Keeper hangar.

The Eagles were nested behind the closed bay doors, and Dad would rarely let me peek through for the slightest glimpse of the birds just sitting there. Occasionally, with the sounds of freedom flying overhead and the smell of jet fuel in the air, I'd pop my head in the door and see the crews working on America's overhead freedom fighters.

After everyone else left the shop, Dad would sometimes open those heavenly doors, take me by the hand, walk me right up to an F-15, to let me climb the ladder into the cockpit. Imagine the excitement in the mind of a 10-year-old growing up in the '80s (right across from Russia), and sitting in a fighter jet. I'm sure it would be just as exciting today.

OMG, I'm going to sit in an F-15! My friends won't believe it, and it's going to be rad! I thought, as I climbed up the ladder to the lowest-bidder-made fighter jet.

There is a smell that can come only from an electric shop and airplane hanger. From what I'm told, it's the smell of ozone, and to me, it's unmistakable. It smells like ball-bearing grease, WD-40, and jet fuel, and it always reminds me of Dad and his scruffy-ass, lamb chops of freedom. It is the smell of heroes.

I stepped into the cockpit, and the first thing I saw was the fighter pilot's joystick. I sat down and took in the same view of the same control panel, and gripped the same joystick as those fighter pilots did.

After a few seconds, I thought, *This is it? This thing looks like scrap metal! This doesn't look anything like what I saw in The Last Starfighter. How boring. This must be low-bid work. Meh. It's just dull, gray metal, and why in the world are there pedals in a plane? Is it a stick shift? Whatever, I'm done. This is boring.*

Not wanting to seem ungrateful, I didn't say anything to my dad except, "Thank you! That was totally rad." I know, I know—what a little turd I was.

Since he was an electrician, Dad had to replace some of the electrical components of the plane, like a faulty joystick. Instead of throwing defective parts in an Air Force-approved dumpster *after* documentation procedures (standard disposal protocol in the Air Force), he decided to skip all the paperwork, bring the joystick home, and give it to me. Let me tell you, that was the absolute coolest thing a little boy could ever get from his dad—a real-life joystick from an F-15. I felt just like Spiff.

That's when it became my dream to become a fighter pilot when I grew up. My mom said I was too fat and short and the Air Force wouldn't want me. Nothing like Latina reverse psychology. I guess life had other plans for me.

But for a moment, there he was: My father, born from the streets of Los Angeles, now standing under the Chugach Mountain Range at Elmendorf Air Force Base in Anchorage, in charge of a squad of iron eagle electricians, in the largest city, of biggest state, in the most power country, on the most advanced planet in the solar system, helping defend America from Mikial Gorbachav's USSR, and the evil Russian boxer. This is the stuff a boys dreams are made of.

I'll never forget how each of those soldiers always listened to and respected my father (who was a civilian then) in that electric shop, and the special salute the guards gave him each time he drove through the main gate. "Wow," I thought. "My pops must be a pretty important guy." He told me about a special salute they gave to him as he drove on base. I don't recall what kind of salute it was though.

And, as far as that rad joystick he gave me, I had that thing all the way through college before I forgot about it in the basement of my ex-girlfriend's house in 1997. That's one of my few regrets: I left my joystick and my VHS tape of La Bamba, never to be seen again.

LESSON:

Boys who love and honor their fathers will in turn have an incredibly awesome time raising their own children. I didn't become a pilot, but I'll be damned if my boys don't work out every day, love '70s rock, end each sentence with sir or ma'am, and are respectful to women. That's a lot more important to me than them becoming an aviator.

CHAPTER 7

MY TWO BROTHERS NAMED RAYMOND

"*H*i, *I'm Charles. This is my brother Raymond, and my other brother named Raymond.*"

I didn't meet any of my dad's immediate family until 1984 when I was 10 years old. My dad told me some of his sisters and two children were flying up to Alaska to come and visit us. I was a little nervous because this would be the first time I would meet any of them. Before they arrived he said to me, "Kid, if your Aunt Vivian says jump, you say 'How high and when can I come down?' You got it?" It wasn't a question. Everyone should have an Aunt Vivian.

We all met for the first time on the mouth of the Willow where my dad and I had always gone in the summers to fish for Kings. Dad and I arrived and set up camp the night before. The rest of the Gonzales clan arrived the next morning in an RV they had rented after their flight landed from L.A. at Anchorage International Airport.

They made the 75-mile trek north to the town of Willow, hopped in the aluminum-weld, flat-bottom river boat, and Captain Butch delivered a boat full of Mexicans about three miles upstream. It was a sight to see.

I still remember meeting my Auntie Vivian for the first time and asking her, "Auntie, who is that other guy over there getting out of the boat?"

"Charles, that's your brother, Raymond."

"What in the name of *George Foreman? You've got to be kidding me!"*

See, I already had a brother named Raymond, from my mother's first marriage. My dad also had one from his first marriage, and now I have two brothers named Raymond, which always makes me feel like a candidate for the short bus and lots of therapy.

Having two brothers named Raymond is something I don't lead with during most conversations, but it's always funny to see the look on people's faces when I tell them.

"Whaaaat?" The first date might say.

Or, "That explains a lot," the group of buddies will say.

"Okay, that will do it. Nice to meet you. Have a nice life," usually the date's next and final words to me.

At least it's a unique selling point to be remembered by.

We spent the weekend getting to know each other as we sat on the riverbanks and next to our campfire. My father also had a daughter named Rochelle, and she and Raymond seemed to share a full-blooded connection that I never had with anyone. Still, they were family, and I was happy to finally meet them.

When Captain Butch returned as scheduled to load up the northern-most group of Los-Angelo-Mexicanos on Sunday afternoon, his airboat broke down on the Willow as he took us upstream back to our car and the RV they rented. There we were, stranded in the middle of Willow, Alaska on a tiny island of river rock, all huddled together like giant, five-foot tall penguins. If there was reality TV back then, the dramatic music would start, with the camera zooming in on each of our frightened brown faces, (except mine) then quickly cutting out to a commercial for reliable boat motors.

Plus, we were stranded right next to a polar bear's cave, and near the spawning grounds of a pod of orcas that were there for the same reason we were—to feast on salmon.

What do you call four Mexicans in a sinking boat? *Cuatro sinko!* LOL! (I can say that because my last name gives me a get out of jail free/uncancellable card when telling Mexican jokes).

The Gonzales clan came up for about 10 days and we traveled all across the state in the rented RV. I didn't grow up around too much family in Alaska, so for me, traveling in an RV full of Mexicans from L.A. was a riot. When I say, "All around the state," I mean north and south. There's basically one road that goes up and down the middle of Alaska. I think I've only seen about .00001% of the state.

Eventually, when we finally returned to Anchorage, I woke up early in the morning without waking anyone and left quietly to go back to the trailer with my mother. When everyone else woke up and noticed I was gone, they asked my father if he knew where I had gone. He quickly called my mother to ask if she had heard from me.

"Yea, Chuck, he's here with me. He walked here this morning from your apartment."

"Why in the hell did he do that?" He asked.

"BECAUSE OF YOUR DAMN DRINKING!" She yelled.

Some things I don't tolerate, even as a child, and staying around a drunken and obnoxious parent was one of them. I'd had enough of his drunken binge and making a fool out of himself. It was so embarrassing for me. Nope, I was done and even as a ten year old child couldn't wait to put that lifestyle behind me. I wasn't wise for my age, I was just scared becoming that type of person myself. Plus, a child feels alone—no, rather a child feels *lonely* when their parent bathes in an intoxicating pool of liquor, then sits for the entire day on the banks of the River Hangover.

After a few days of his thick-tongued, droopy-eyed inebriation, I'd decided to go my own way silently and remove myself from an uncomfortable situation. I loved my dad too much to keep seeing him like that day after day. Funny, my family still talks about how I left on that vacation years ago.

I'm not close with Raymond. I'm not close with the other Raymond either. But I am close with my father's daughter, Rochelle. We have some eerie similarities that only genetics can explain since we grew up thousands of miles apart. We like things our own way, we try to protect our kids from the cycle of generational alcoholism, we both have college degrees and value education and intelligence, and we're both lightweights when it comes to drinking. Finally, we both have awesome curly hair. It's like we have the same dad or something. And strangely, we both have really friggin' tall kids over 6'-2". Must be some kind of recessive gene that skips a generation. Damn.

LESSON:

When you do good, like bringing part of your massive family to Alaska, your kindness will be rewarded. Dad's reward was creating a connection between my family and me that is incredibly strong to this day. Were it not for the kindness and generosity of my father, I would have never met my other brother named Raymond. *George Foreman 1949–2025. Rest in peace, you good and faithful servant.

CHAPTER 8

THE ANATOMY OF SHARED CUSTODY

*W*hen you're a Dad with an ex-wife and two weekends a month with your kid, you just have to do the best with what you've got.

My parents separated and divorced sometime around 1983. A mean alcoholic and a happy alcoholic do not co-exist very well and it was certainly time for that relationship to end before someone was killed. My dad moved out of the trailer and into an apartment a few miles away from us, and per the judge's decision, I assume made with the influence of a beautiful, blond-haired, five-foot-tall Latina, I was only allowed to see him every other weekend. I wasn't sure at the time why I could only see the man I looked up to twice a month. In fact, I wouldn't discover why until over 40 years later (I write more about this in story #40. 'I'm Still Pissed').

Children of divorced parents never have an easy childhood, especially if the parents are not great, post-divorce co-parents. The scheduling, pick up, drop off, phone calls, sports practices and game time—it's always an ordeal, and something I never wanted to have my own children experience. And God forbid if a child support payment is a day late . . . all hell breaks loose. It's a turmoil a person never forgets, and without personal development, purposeful growth and daily enrichment, the memories of being a child of divorce can haunt a person for a lifetime.

The keystones these days of any divorce with children are state-mandated courses, asset allocations, custody awards, parenting time including 2-2-5s, one-week-on-week-off, major holidays, summer vacations, Father's Day, Mother's Day, birthdays, additional vacations, and let's not forget, the child support. The support that some mothers hold over dads, dads who just want to see their children. Not all mothers are saints, and they can treat children like hostages, holding them ransom until the 1st of the month when that check comes in. Then, visitation is only allowed by the prescription written, not a minute more, and definitely not a minute less. Lastly fathers, don't expect to see a line-item expense sheet of how your child support is spent, especially by an alcoholic in a trailer. No one wants to show how much the local night clubs are being subsidized by child support.

Subsequently, it's helpful if the alcoholic parent can recount what was agreed to in the divorce decree, which usually doesn't happen very often. Instead, it's the clear-minded child who is still developing new neural pathways and habits who becomes the mediator between the two hazy parents. And let me tell you something, there ain't a snowball's chance in hell I'd be the one to forget what weekend I was supposed to be with my father. That was my ticket out of hell twice per month.

Divorce decrees and parenting plans always force parents to make the least-bad decision for their children. Sometimes divorce is necessary to keep a bad situation from getting worse, and though it may be the least-bad decision, the grass isn't always greener on the other side. The hearts of children are inevitably broken, sides are often chosen by children, and sometimes animosity is piled high for years, until it causes an avalanche of emotional turmoil and breakdown. Divorce is a burnt hole in the fabric of the family, but as I said, and as the judge in my own divorce said, "Creating new traditions are what's most important for you to make with your kids now that you're divorced, Mr. Gonzales."

And BTW, if the grass *is* greener on the other side:

1. There's the possibility of a septic tank leak unknown to the owner, or;
2. You're a shitty gardener.

After the divorce decree was signed, I was always filled with excitement when my dad picked me up in his tricked-out, yellow Monte Carlo with the gold rims. The car and the fun we'd have didn't matter though; I just wanted to hang out with my pops. He just wanted to make sure we had a good time and that I was entertained and fed. He did a great job creating new traditions too.

In the '80s, it was easy for kids to be entertained, and on our divorced-mandated weekends, our things were:

1. Going to the movies. With the exception of:
   a. *Scarface*. Bad decision on his part. We walked out about 10 minutes after it started, and;
   b. *Kiss Of The Spider Woman*. I can only imagine he thought it was a superhero movie. Uh, nope. Ten minutes, tops, and we were gone.
2. Chuck-E-Cheese. We had a big, two-story Chuck-E-Cheese in Anchorage. I don't know how they were set up in the lower 48

during the '80s, but in a genius move for revenue, they served beer on tap for parents, pizza, and played classic oldies on animatronics, which was perfect for my dad. I LOVED the pizza and he loved the endless beer and classic rock music.

Chuck-E-Cheese had separate music rooms, one with a giant animatronic lion that sang Elvis songs, another with dogs that sang Beetles songs, and I think another one with a big, lady chicken that sang Dolly Parton songs. Dad usually brought a book to read, had a few pitchers of beer, and kept a stack of quarters on his table. I'm sure if there was an animatronic arctic fox, dressed as a mariachi and singing sad Mexican songs, Dad would have seen his life savings dwindle even farther, quarter by quarter.

When you're a divorced parent trying to entertain your child that you only see twice per month, you have to be pretty creative to keep the kid(s) occupied and excited. There's no shortage of things to do with your child, which is why my dad just tried his best to be adventurous, by taking me downhill skiing, cross-country skiing, inter tubing down Campbell Creek River in Anchorage, camping, fishing, shooting, bowling, snow-machining, and swimming. There is no greater respect I have than for a divorced parent who wants to be part of his child's life, going out of their way to re-create the future and build new memories.

He'd give me a handful of tokens for the video games, which would last me about 30 minutes. I'd always find him just listening to Elvis or Beatles songs, plugging tokens into the mini-jukebox at his table, and picking tunes he grew up with as a kid. I never saw him in the lady chicken room though.

"Here you go, kid. Here's some more tokens, and don't spend them too fast!" I'd be back in another 10 minutes, and his pitcher was a little lighter. Back then I was a regular arcade jockey, but it was always the most super funnest when he played with me.

My boys these days ask, "Dad, what did games did you and Papa Chuck play on the weekends when you could only see him twice a month?"

- Dragon's Lair
- Galaga
- Return of the Jedi
- Frogger
- Defender
- Donkey Kong
- Teenage Mutant Ninja Turtles
- Track & Field
- Dig Dug

I never liked Joust, Q*Bert, Gauntlet, or Tron. I feel like those were for kids who'd grow up to be Dungeons & Dragons cosplayers. The same ones who would grow up to be those wealthy, Tesla-driving, software engineer, self-described nerds. I'm just jealous, that's all.

And the Chuck-E-Cheese pizza. I don't know what it was about their pizza, but I could eat that for breakfast, lunch, and dinner. I think I did, which is how I got so chunky when I was a kid. Dad would remind me of it too.

If we were walking around town and he'd see an overweight dude, he might look at me and *jokingly* say, "See him, kid? That's what you'll look like if you don't stop eating!" LOL! He had a humorous delivery about it though—never condescending.

Calm down, Karen. It was true, and funny. Plus, I think it worked.

After I drained him of all quarters and tokens, we'd leave. Then we'd stop by the local butcher shop for another tradition, Mr. Prime Beef meat market, to pick up a second dinner (after the pizza). My God, I loved that place. It was always the same for us—just a couple of T-bone steaks.

Then, we'd stop by the VHS and beta video rental store and walk the aisles of:

Drama

Comedy

Family (lame)

Thriller

and our favorite,

Horror. We loved watching horror movies together.

"Be kind, rewind!" some of the tapes said. I remember he had a top-of-the-line VHS player in the early '80s, too.

Sunday was for football, with a lot of yelling at the TV, and inevitably, the moment I dreaded—I had to go back home to my mothers (Lord, the hair on my arms stands up just thinking about her and that damn tin can trailer).

I hated nothing more than driving into that grim, muddy-ass, trailer park on Sunday nights, knowing I would have to endure a full two weeks before I could escape again to Chuck-E.-Cheese and Mr. Prime Beef. As they say, easy times make weak men, and no good sailor was ever made in a safe harbor.

LESSON:

If you don't gather anything when you're young, you won't find anything when you're old. I can only pray the gratitude I gathered on those weekends with my dad is handed down to my boys during my own divorce-mandated weekends. Having awesome, respectful, grandkids with two parents who stay married, that's my goal for my boys.

CHAPTER 9

"HONK AT FLOYD!"

We lived at Top Hand Trailer Court at 2409 McRae Road, Space 22, Anchorage, Alaska, 99123. That place was so evil it permanently seared its address forever into my mental file cabinet. A "special" part of town, it still had somewhat illegal—let's say, houses of ill repute. It was certainly entertaining to live there.

Dad was the lucky one. When he and my mom divorced, he moved into a new place a few miles away. I was stuck in a mouse-infested, crushed beer can with the other hoodrat kids of divorced parents in Top Hand Trailer Court. We all dressed in worn-out shoes, torn jeans, and dirty shirts, with runny noses from riding our beat-up BMX bikes in the cold, everywhere.

Behind the trailer park was the infamous API Community House. Oh, what's API, you ask?

Alaska . . .

Psychiatric . . .

Institute . . .

API housed some really interesting people. They weren't criminals, but "low-risk" patients, with mental health disabilities, assessed safe enough to be released to live on their own in the community, with minimal supervision. This was fascinating for a child to watch and it put a giant, "WTF" question mark on a continual, repeat loop in my head. As kids in the '80s, we were told never to speak to strangers, let alone strangers who lived at API. As a result we never knew their names so we had to be creative when seeing them on the street. We called one man Wolfman Jack, because he was super hairy. Another was "Mr. Pregnant," because he thought he was pregnant. Not like the new age men in Portland today who try to get pregnant and nurse babies, this guy really thought he was pregnant. He had a big beer belly, and he always walked around in this red, polyester jacket that was two times too small for him and rode up on his stomach.

And then there was Floyd . . .

If you lived in Anchorage in the '80s and '90s, you will forever remember Floyd. The guy was legendary.

Floyd was a happy-go-lucky Native Alaskan who lived at API. He was mentally challenged, but deep down inside, he knew exactly what was going on. Nearly every day, Floyd stood at the intersection of Minnesota and Spenard with a cardboard sign that just read:

"HONK AT FLOYD!"

And you know what? People honked the shit out of their horns at Floyd, with no reticence. He just stood out there for hours, with a *huge* smile on his face, jumping up and down, rain or shine, waving at everyone who drove by. The guy's energy was incredible, and he was having a good time at the game of life. All damn day he'd be out there—only one care in the world: To make himself and the people around him happy.

My sister and her boyfriend worked up the road at a fast food joint for a spell, and occasionally I'd visit them for a free burger and to say hi. Every once in a while, Floyd was in there when I stopped by, always cycling through his fast-food routine:

1. Sit by himself at a table with a cup of soda.
2. Take a sip through the straw.
3. Quickly point to and under his breath, count the bubbles on the surface of the soda.
4. Put his hands together, close his eyes, quickly say a prayer, and give thanks.
5. Open his eyes, take another sip, and repeat this process until his drink was gone. Again, fascinating, just fascinating for a 10-year-old to watch.

On one of my weekends with Dad, we drove past Floyd on his usual street corner. Happy as always, with his big perpetual smile, Floyd jumped up and down, waved to the cars that drove by, and held his sign.

Noticing I was staring at Floyd, Dad turned his head to glance at me sitting in the passenger seat and said, "Kid, what would you think of me if I just stood out there and held a sign like Floyd on the street corner?"

I don't remember what I told him. I probably said I thought it would be fine, as long as he was happy. But what I really thought and felt was (and I still feel the same today), *"How much different grown-ups must be, looking at others and seeing all the crazy, instead of seeing the happy."* Grown-ups are so judgy sometimes. Maybe it's our human nature to see what's wrong before we see actually understand what's right with them. Why couldn't Dad just be happy for Floyd?

But the joke was on Dad and the rest of us. Turns out, Floyd knew exactly what he was doing, and eventually he dipped his toes in entrepreneurial waters.

Instead of "Honk At Floyd," he changed his advertising and his product placement location. He wrote a sign that read:

"GIVE FLOYD MONEY"

Then, he stood in front of our local grocery store on Spenard road instead of on the street corner. Wouldn't you know it, people threw money at that guy.

But the police eventually showed up when they got word of Floyd's new, lucrative business model.

"Floyd, man, you can't be doing this. It's illegal to panhandle."

Floyd, not being as slow and mentally challenged as everyone thought he was, decided to make the trek downtown to city hall, and wouldn't you know it, he got a damn business license, with "panhandling" as his occupation! I kid you not!

Floyd ran straight back to the grocery store, held out his sign and his business license, and wouldn't you know it, people started throwing money at him again.

A few hours later, the po-po showed up, but Floyd provided his business license, making him a legit businessman now, and straight-up gangsta'. "Yeah, Floyd, that's not going to fly in front of a judge. If we come out here again, we'll have to arrest you."

Like any good businessman, he had to adjust. Same location, new advertising tactic: **"Floyd can't ask you for money, but you can give it to me if you want to."**

It was kind of a mouthful, but apparently, that did the trick. The police no longer showed up, and Floyd had a modest, secondary income stream.

Floyd died about 15 years ago. I wonder if he and my dad are up there together, jumping, waving, and holding up signs for souls who pass by, "Honk at Chuck and Floyd!" That actually sounds like something my dad would do. Maybe the joke was on all of us after all.

LESSON:

Don't be afraid to learn about your neighbors. Looks can be deceiving and they might be wiser than you give them credit for. As the old adage goes, "don't judge a book by it's cover." Floyd was an entrepreneur before I ever even thought about becoming one.

CHAPTER 10

CHASING TURKEYS AND RACKING UP 9-BALL

O*ne thing about my dad, homeboy was a strangely good bowler.*

Some of the traditions my dad and I made were: 1) Bowling and; 2) Pool. I never, *never, ever, ever, ever* beat my dad at bowling. During my divorced-weekends I was allotted to spend with him, we could sometimes be found at the Center Bowl in Anchorage for cheap fun in the winter. We didn't bowl much in the summertime because each weekend was filled with fishing and camping. But in the winter, I could spend hours upon hours sitting in that bowling alley with him, *never* getting bored. (Funny, I could always sit with him next to a fire and never get bored either.)

For my birthday, he bought me my own, blue, 10-pound bowling ball, with the name "Charlie" engraved on it, along with a blue bowling-ball bag, a pair of bowling shoes, a wrist brace, and a polishing rag. I was the Big-Little Chuckowski. LOL! If I was

Big-Little Chuckowski, Dad was the Chunky God Of Thunder. That's actually a pretty accurate description.

I have zero idea where Mr. Saturday Night Chops learned how to bowl, but he had the "curved-arch-of-death" when he threw his 16-pound cannonball. Even now, a 16-pounder seems heavy to me. I don't think it will ever feel light, no matter how many days a week I deadlift, bench press, and squat, because only my father was strong enough to lift and throw that thing. Maybe I'm just not worthy enough to lift it.

He also had everything a studly bowler needed: The sexy ball formed in the heart of a dying star, bowling shoes, hand resin, a wrist wrap, sweat cloth, and a credit card on file at the bar. I remember he always looked so damn tall, standing there on the little brown triangles atop the maple hardwood, as he loaded up his right arm, took a three steps, pulled the trigger, and shot the cannon ball from the barrel.

"Boom!" Strike.

Another *"Boom!"* Strike.

Then, *"Bang!"* Open frame and a spare. No turkey. Santa Maria!

We bowled in the '80s, when you had to keep track of your own score with golf pencils stashed in the little silver containers, inset on the scorekeeper's table with the overhead projection screen. We were just outside the cusp of the digital age, but I thought it was a golden age. I still do.

When I tell people I grew up bowling with my father they always ask me one question: "Can you break a hundred?"

I thought that was so funny, because I was always chasing 200. I usually ended somewhere between 150-180. But Dad—well he was a 200+ point kind of bowler. I may never fully know how he became such a damn good bowler, and it's a mystery that will forever be lost with the ages, like his lambchops. As hard as I tried, I could never beat him.

He liked to keep me occupied and humble while we were together every other weekend. He usually out-fished me, out-bowled me, and out-pooled me. (I just make words up sometimes.)

When he was tired of whooping my butt at bowling, we'd rack 'em up at River City Billiards, and he'd spank me like a red-headed grandchild (his grandchild, my middle son, happens to be a redhead).

We'd both carefully choose our house sticks, roll them across the table to see if they were warped, and pick the least wobbly one to use. I liked a 19-ounce stick. Dad liked the 21. Then, his lessons would begin.

"You're little ones, I'm big ones," he'd say.

"Eleven ball, corner pocket. Eighteen ball, side pocket. Eight ball, corner pocket off the bank." He'd call it. He'd nail it.

"Rack 'em, kid!"

What the shit, over. I'd whisper to myself. *He beat me again.*

Games of eight-ball and nine-ball for hours, and of course a few pitchers of beer for him. If we had a friend with us, we always played cut throat. I loved, loved, loved playing pool with him. Eventually, I would become good enough to beat him, sometimes.

"Kid, the longer you play, the better you get. The more I play, the worse I get."

There's a lesson in there somewhere.

Once again, I have no idea how he was so damn good at pool. How did he have time to get so good at pool *and* bowling *and* fishing? That guy must have skipped more school than I could ever imagine. There was no amount of cheating I could get away with that was as good a substitute as practice itself. But when did he have time to master caroming?

FAST FORWARD TO 2023

When I was blessed with three boys of my own, our hometown had no pool halls. As it turns out, they're terrible, god-awful, horrific, appalling, horrendous, pool players. I took them all to a pool hall recently in San Antonio, and well, it was just embarrassing. They aimed their pool sticks using the top of the knuckles, for god's sake!

"Dad, what's 9-ball?"

I've failed as a father, I thought. My god, it took an eternity to explain that game to them.

"Cutthroat? What's cutthroat?" they asked.

I tried to explain it to them, and that's I could feel my soul and patience slowly leaving my body with each of their questions. The next stage of their training as men must begin now. I will show them the *power* of top spin, backspin, and English. Then their training will be complete, and in time, they will call me—Master!

None of us have the bowling ball arch-of-death yet, though. Maybe one day we'll figure it out.

LESSON:

If it pleases The Almighty, we will one day be filled with the Spirit to understand cutthroat, throwing a bowling ball along the arch of power, and knowing how to hold a pool stick like a pro. Please, Almighty—let that day be soon rather than later. The joy and skill are only found in the process of learning, in the relationships and experiences shared, and not who wins one game of 9-ball on the weekend.

CHAPTER 11

SNOW-MACHEENS AND THE IDITAROD

*D*ad loved watching the Iditarod. I mean, he had to be the only LA-born Chicano who loved to watch dog mushing.

Iditarod is a 1,100-mile, dogsled race over the tundra of Alaska, and it's one of the things I love and miss about that place. These days, the starting line is in downtown Anchorage for media coverage during Fur Rondezvous (an outdoor carnival in February), and the finish line is 1,100 miles northwest in the town of Nome (Texas is only 800 miles from the southern-most to the northern-most tip). Yes, there is an outdoor carnival in *February*, in *Alaska*. It features rides, games, fur traders, reindeer, and *massive* snow sculptures big enough to climb and slide down. Sub-zero carnivals are pretty damn fun for a kid.

We wouldn't always watch the race at the starting line in downtown Anchorage. Dad would eventually build a house in the middle of BFE, 60 miles north of Anchorage in a town called Knik. As it turned out, the Iditarod re-starting point was just a few miles north of his house. Each year, we'd hop on our snow machines, pulling trailers loaded with snacks and booze, and race through the Alaskan wilderness to set up camp on the frozen Seven-Mile Lake to watch "The Last Great Race" in person.

For reference, Alaskans call snow mobiles "snow machines." But Alaskan-Mexicans call them "SNOW MACHEENS!" A Mexican accent and an exclamation point are always required too. Try saying it right now. Fun, isn't it?

We'd always have a fire right on the frozen lake. The ice was so thick it would never fully melt. We'd unload the supplies and set up camp while we were waiting for the mushers to arrive. To pass the time, we'd jump on our snow machines and open them up on the frozen lake. I learned 110–115 mph is a special kind of fun when you're on flat snow and ice.

The mushers would start coming in during the late afternoon/ early evening. This left *plenty* of time for the adults to tie one on before the mushers arrived. I can't believe no one ever fell in the fire, now that I think about it.

"There's another dead soldier!" My dad would yell, as he threw an empty beer bottle in the back of the trailer. To this day I have never heard anyone refer to an empty beer can as a "dead soldier."

"Hey, kid! Bring me another *cerveza!*"

"Hey, Chuck! Throw me another trail soda!" someone would yell at my dad.

After all the ingestion of barley, hops, and electrolytes, we *definitely* designated a section for yellow snow.

In Alaska, when all is still in the wilderness, it is the most peaceful sound you've never heard. It's the sounds of The Great Land that bring peace to the mind and calmness to the heart. The crackling of the fire on the ice, snow crunching beneath our boots, barking dogs in the distance, and the slicing of the dogsled skis sailing over the snow, and the noises of absolutely nothing are all sounds everyone should hear once in their lifetime.

The sleds became louder as they closed in on our campsite near the edge of Seven-Mile Lake. A dog sled sounds like hockey skates on ice, with the dogs' 48 paws drumming randomly, yet somehow synchronously on the snow. Believe it or not, all the dogs are smiling, and they *love* mushing. As sure as you know your own dog loves you and loves playing fetch, Alaskan Huskies love to mush. It's what they're bred and born to do.

Nighttime started to set in, and some of the mushers would stop their sleds in front of our campsite before they entered the trail back into the frozen forest. They'd check the little fleece-paw booties on their dogs, and give them meds or water, as needed. Sometimes the mushers grabbed a snack for themselves, too. I remember one musher had a stick of butter rolled in sugar and chocolate chips. Another ate a cheesecake each day just for calories. Becoming an Iditarod musher became my new goal, just for the snacks.

Our campsite was sort of an unofficial checkpoint, probably because of the light from roaring fire on the ice, and the mushers knew we'd be some of the last people they'd see for hundreds of miles.

I don't know the dog musher's name, but he parked his sled close to our campsite just off the trail before he reentered the forest. Another musher was coming up fast behind him and wasn't making a pit stop. The parked musher's dogs veered off to the right, directly in front of the oncoming musher's sled, and just like a T-bone car accident, *boom!* Suddenly there was an entangled mess of 24, harnessed dogs, all biting and snarling at each other, tied in a knot like tangled fishing string. I was standing by the fire, wide-eyed, mouth opened, watching the shitshow unfold.

"Hey! Help!" One of the mushers yelled to us.

Uh, yeah, I'm good! I thought, as I stood there and watched (I had a terrible fear of dogs growing up. I was bitten 10 times by dogs in my neighborhood). My dad ran over to help the mushers untangle the knotted mess of dogs. I hadn't grown into my man-courage yet to help them, but I'm sure my dad didn't want me in the middle of the tangled mess anyway.

"Hey, thanks! And don't tell anyone!" The mushers yelled before they returned to the trail in the woods.

In the Iditarod, there can be *no* assistance of any kind, from anyone outside the race. If a musher is caught receiving third-party assistance, he or she is disqualified from the race. I doubt any official was ever notified of Mr. Iditarod Lamb Chops coming to the rescue. I was just happy none of my fingers and toes became Huskey appetizers, and I'd have a hell of a story to tell at school. To this day, some people still don't believe this is a true story. FYI, this is a true story.

When we packed up to head home for the night, we'd always find the little fleece booties along the trail that had fallen off the dog's feet while they were mushing. I used to have a basket full of those things. Now, I don't have a single one. How great would it have been to put one of those little booties in the grave with my father? A doggie bootie from the Iditarod, a pack of Terryton cigarettes, and a bottle of his favorite beer. I'll have to put those on his grave the next time I visit him.

Alaska: Where men are men, and women win the Iditarod. God bless you, Susan Butcher.

LESSON:

1. When a father gives his son a snow macheen, no one can imagine the joy, the freedom, and the stories that can come with it. It wasn't the snow macheen I looked forward to though—it's what the snow macheen showed me all those years ago. For those gifts, I'll always honor my dad.

2. My father always asked me to get him another beer. In an effort to *not* desensitize my children toward alcohol, I vowed to never treat them as my own personal bartenders. They know to never, never hand me a beer, or even get another adult a beer. Parents, get your ass up and get your own beer.

CHAPTER 12

THE MOVIES OF THE '80S

I imagine the '80s in Alaska were probably like the '80s in the Lower 48—but, everything was delayed in Alaska. Movies were always delayed by a few months. New music was always delayed, and football games are still delayed.

I always had to be careful when I was talking to dad about the score of the Rams' games because they weren't on TV yet in Alaska. "Don't tell me the damn final score! I'm still watching the game!" He'd yell at me over the phone when I called on Sundays.

I imagine growing up in Alaksa during that product-placement, low-rent CGI age wasn't much different than what kids experienced in the lower 48. For us, it was just colder, darker, and delayed.

To this day, I can still remember how excited I was to watch *anything jedi or comando related* with my dad on one of my designated weekends with him. My dad was a gigantic, goofball kid his entire life, and I think he liked going to the movies with me just as much as I loved going with him.

He picked me up on a Saturday morning, and I was bursting at the seams with excitement. Literally, I was a chucky-ass monkey, so I was bursting out of the top button of my jeans.

"Well, what do you want to do this weekend, kid?" He said.

"*What!* Dad, you know what we're doing! We're going to the movies!"

Dad took me to Denali Theater movie theater in Anchorage to watch what was happening in a galaxy far, far away. Dad *always* sat on the very edge of whichever row we chose, I think so he could high tail it out of the movie theater and beat everyone out of the parking lot. I bet he would have sat at the edge of the pew too if we ever went to Mass together. Guess I'll never know.

SIDENOTE: Alaskans pronounce it Den-alley. Whenever we hear someone say DEN-AH-LEE, we know they're from the lower 48 and watched too many Discovery Channel shows. Every time I hear it on a commercial for a full-sized SUV, I just want to throw a damn ulu at the TV, and beat the radio with an usik! (You can discover these and other Alaskan adages in the glossary of terms at the end of this book.) It's "Den-al-lee!" Not "Den-oll-ee!"

Before we went to the movie theater, we had to first make our traditional stop to pick up a few quarter pounders with cheese. Dad would buy about 10 friggin' cheeseburgers and we'd stuff them into our big-ass, poofy, winter, Alaskan jackets before we walked inside the movie theater.

After we picked our seats and the trailers started, we'd discreetly unwrap Ray Crock's middle-of-the road crown jewel. Seriously, we wolfed down four or five of those apiece. I'm still trying to burn off that baby fat to this day.

I'm sure the sound of those wrappers and the smell of cheeseburgers annoyed the hell out of each person we sat next to in every movie theater. Too bad, being sneaky was fun for me and pops.

The movies of the '80s were everything they were hyped up to be, and it's funny how my kids ask me about what it was like going back then. "Were they color, or black and white?"

"What the shit, over? I'm not that old!" All children think their parents are ancient and always discount the accomplishments of what previous generations achieved.

Sometimes Dad would take me swimming the next day at the West High School pool to burn off a few calories from the day before (just FYI, as Certified Strength & Conditioning Specialist, a CrossFit Coach and a USA Weightlifting coach, burning off 4 cheeseburgers by swimming one hour is and always will be absolutely impossible). But then, he'd just buy me a strawberry dipped ice cream cone when we finished—which was actually my favorite part of swimming. In fact, he never taught me how to swim, he just watched me hold on to the wall and scooch all the way down the edge of the pool while he swam laps and jumped off the diving board.

If there's one thought I still have each time I drive past that soft-serve ice cream haven it's how my old man took me swimming on Sundays and single-handedly helped me put on a thick layer of "protective Alaskan insulation" to endure what would be the coldest years of my life at the University of Alaska, Fairbanks. Maybe he knew what he was doing after all.

I absolutely love going to the movies with my boys these days. In 2016, *Creed* and *The Force Awakens* were both released in movie theaters. My heart nearly exploded with excitement, and I couldn't wait to take my boys out of school to see both films. I'm sure my dad felt the same way when he took me to the movies. He and I are both big kids at heart.

I bought tickets online for all of us to watch *The Force Awakens*, then drove over to pick up all the boys from school in the middle of the day to stand in line outside of the movie theater, telling them stories of how my father and I did the same thing some 30 years earlier.

Since I was a trainer and a gym owner at the time, we skipped the quarter pounder cheeseburgers, but we did manage to sneak in a few chocolates from the dollar store.

Full disclosure: The boys were getting really tired of me pulling them out of school early to see *Creed* three times and three times to see *The Force Awakens*. I'd do it all over again because at the end of the day, I don't remember a lick of English class from the fifth grade, but I do remember standing in line with my dad at a theater in Anchorage. That's way more important than not ending a sentence in a preposition, isn't it?

By the way, "Hoth" is Alaskan Athabaskan for "Fairbanks," which is where the icy snow scenes were filmed when the Galactic Empire attacked the rebel alliance, just over the hill from the UAF campus. If you look in the background during the movie, you can see the UAF main campus just over the hills.

LESSON:

Harmony among family is delightful, pleasing to the eyes of the Almighty. I hope Dad's happy that I pulled my boys out of school so often to enjoy a matinee because I'm too cheap for the night time showings.

CHAPTER 13

GUNS AND ALCOHOL: A TERRIBLE COCKTAIL

A lot of my stories seem to involve alcohol. Bad decisions make for great stories—and hopefully a good book, too.

Blending families is really, really hard. My dad tried to do it in 1974 with my mother, who already had three kids of her own in a single-wide trailer, on a muddy dirt road. I can still remember the smell of that road, and that's still the first thing I think of when I smell the rain, how blended families can fail.

Three kids were already living with our mother in a trailer before my dad and I came along. We even had pet cockatoo and a poor dog named Diamond, terminally tied up outside all year long with a chain around his neck, tangled in fur. I'll never forget how badly I felt for that dog.

I think my brothers and sisters all hated each other, and their intemperate anger toward my father prevented any type of familial and empathetic connection. They were part of that older, Gen-X generation—the mean ones that grew their hair out, drove muscle cars and got in fights all the time.

One day within to confines of the trailer, my older brother was irate with one of my sisters for some reason, chased her with a butterknife around the house, then threw it as hard as he could as she ran away from him down the hall to her bedroom. *Wham!* Right in her butt!

I don't know how hard you have to throw a butter knife at someone to have it stick in their butt cheek, but it must be pretty damn hard. Years later, I heard she still had the scar.

Poor Dad. That guy had to endure three a-hole kids who didn't like him; an alcoholic, angry, 4' 11" Mexican wife, a pet cockatoo, and a new born son. What a glutton for punishment he was.

Dad and Mom were a bad mixture of alcohol and cigarettes: A *bad* alcoholic, and one *"happy"* alcoholic. Like Isacc Newton said, "A negative times a positive equals a negative." Okay, maybe it wasn't Issacc Newton, but you know what I mean.

I don't mean to imply there's anything such as a positve, or "good alcoholic," and there's no romanticizing addiction. A noxious transformation definitely happens when alcohol hits some people's bloodstream, and that makes a "bad" alcoholic. This is why most villages in Alaska are "dry, or damp." (more on that later in chapter #20, Smuggling Canadian Whiskey.) The concupiscence of alcoholism runs deeper than a Jimi Hendrix album in Alaska and within the confines of my entire family. Real, real deep.

As an adult, it's easier for me to understand why 12-packs of pilsner beer, whiskey and rum were staples in our house back then. Alcohol offers the promise to:

"Take the edge off."

"Hide the reality of bills."

"Cover the problems of life."

"Create smiles and happiness."

"Make people more ingratiating."

"Provide a well-earned escape of reality for the night after a hard days work."

In my professional opinion, these are all chickenshit, bullshit, and horseshit excuses, all rolled into one smoking pile of dogshit, to alleviate the responsibility of maturity, to purposefully avoid being a decent parent with standards for morality. If there's one thing I cannot stand, it's making excuses. Booze is just an excuse to stay child-like as Peter Pan and never grow up. It's what I call a "mood enhancer." If you're cool, you think it makes you cooler. If you're angry, it definitely makes you angrier. If you're sad, it makes you much sadder.

And, if you're Mexican, it makes you Mas Mexicano. That means listening to sad songs about broken hearts and cheating women, becoming really angry with your cousins, and getting a hankering for menudo and tacos at 2 a.m. This is 1000 percent true.

In my experience, only one "good" can possibly emerge from children raised by alcoholic parents: Some children experience a darkness that they will avoid at every turn and will protect their own children from at all costs. It's why I never ask my boys to get me a beer. Yes, this is a fear which my ego tries to protect me against, and I'm sure it's the cause of some kind of personal growth. Maybe I'll address that in my next book.

Why on God's green earth would anyone willingly expose children to the flames of hell? No, exposing children to evil does not make them anti-fragile and stronger. As parents we are to protect the children in our garden from thorns and weeds. When their roots are a little deeper, then we start exposing them to the elements of this world. But there's a time and a place, and as far as I can tell, that time is not during childhood.

Otherwise, nothing, and I mean *nothing* good comes from living with alcoholic parents. One always blames the other (there's no accountability with alcoholics), the only communicating is yelling to make sure they're heard at all costs (there's no actual listening, just yelling). There's very little agreement, and they can't wait for kids to go to bed and be out of their hair for the night (yeah screw that, I love hanging out with my kids whenever I can). Plus, the whole trailer always seemed to be redolent with the aroma seaping from their pores. Another smell I'll never forget.

In 1982, that entire Alcoholics-R-Us situationship culminated into the end of their marriage and me seeing my dad only every-other weekend for the next eight years.

Dad came home from work at midnight. He worked the swing shift on Elmendorf Air Force Base in Anchorage. Mom had already tied one on by the time he arrived home that night.

Mom dragged me out of bed by grabbing me by the hair and pulling me out into the single-wide living room in front of my dad, who was sitting peacefully on the couch with a drink and watching TV. The sluring alcoholic began browbeating my father, and didn't relent. This memory is seared in my soul.

Shaking my head with a fist-full of my hair in her grip, she yelled, *"Look at what your drinking is doing to him! You're making him cry!"*

'What the hell, lady? No I'm not! You're making him cry—shaking the shit out of him and grabbing his hair! Let him go and put him back to bed!" He said. I just wiggled away and curled up on the couch.

She accused him of cheating on her, and she threw every damn thing that wasn't tied down in the house at him. Pots, pans, eggs, potatoes, butter knives—if it was related to cooking, she threw it at dad. And guess who had to clean up the dried eggs on the wall the next day? Can you imagine having eggs thrown at you at midnight by a little drunken Latina, right when you get home from work? *Aye caramba* . . .

For whatever reason, Dad had thought it would be a really good idea to buy mom a gun for protection while he was at work. Three crazy step kids, one eight-year-old (me), and an alcoholic Latina at home. Not one of my dad's better decisions. The yelling escalated. Then it became physical. She pushed, punched, shoved, and as always, tried to grab the hair on the back of his head. Then Mom finally went for the gun. Mind you, I was watching all of this curled up in a ball on the couch. She ran into their bedroom, grabbed the .22 caliber handgun, pointed it with both hands right at my dad, and with a scared and shaking voice yelled, *"I'm gonna shoot you, Chuck!"*

Tears filled her eyes, and I still remember the sadness on her face as she pointed the gun straight at my father. I'll never forget that look of terror on his face, just a few feet away from where I was curled up on the couch. No son should ever see his dad that terrified. His eyes widend, his mouth dropped, he gasped in shock, in terror, and slowly raised his hands. He lunged at her before she could pull the trigger, ripping the gun from her hands, and threw her to the bed, where I could only hear her sobbing. I'm pretty sure they just made love afterwards and called it a night. It just doesn't get more Mexican than this.

There was a saying in Anchorage around that time: A Spenard Divorce. That's when a woman would shoot her husband to speed up the divorce process. I shit you not. There was no Spenard Divorce that night.

I went to sleep on the couch and woke to get myself ready for the second grade the next morning. Learning to cope as a product of alcoholic parents and the intentional growth I found is a topic for another book I am in no way qualified to write.

What happened to me? I turned out to be a terible student. I couldn't focus lost interest in most topics. There wasn't much which ever interested me though the 12th grade, and I never saw how kids could place any importance on education when I was just trying to survive. More about that in story #17, Atonement.

Sidenote: I cannot speak for all children of alcoholic parents, and birth order likely plays a significant factor in the development and decision-making ability in the child's life. I swore I would never raise my children in that kind of environment, and while I drink moderately and responsibly around them, I sometimes worry I'm too overprotective, too "helicopter-parent" at times. It is what it is.

But I'll never stop pruning those thorns and weeds from my most precious flowers. Soon enough they have their own life to make their own least-bad decisions. God, I just hope they breed with the right woman.

LESSON:

My experiences in poverty, in hate, and in darkness give me nothing to boast about. Yes, offspring can grow to be wicked and disgraceful, but we have a choice to either compartmentalize ourselves as "products of our environment," or we can turn our faces away from darkness and toward the One who calls us home instead.

Even then I knew that the one who listened to God Almighty would be protected. I just don't know why or how I believed it, but, wisdom told me that parents should keeps their guns locked away, separate from the ammunition.

THE CREATION AND THE FALL

The judge didn't even make the least-good decision, that son-of-a-bitch made the best bad decision.

Backstory: *In 2009 while I was still living in Oregon, my stepmother, Wilma, sent me a large envelope with a few letters and the genealogy of my father's family. I didn't pay too much attention to it because I thought it was just memorabilia about our family genealogy. I briefly looked through it and then filed it away for 13 years. On September 6th, 2022, 13 years later, I discovered, just what those letters were.*

When I was growing up in Anchorage, there was about *one* woman for every *four* men. And forget about fashion. Fashion in Alaska meant both socks matched. For the ladies, the odds were good, but for the men, the goods were odd. Yep, it was slim pickings for the men on the tundra, but as luck would have it, that's where my parents met. At a damn dive bar, off the ghetto streets of Spenard in Anchorage. And what was the bar called? Poncho Villa's. Dios mio...

I mean it makes sense. Where else would a Gonzales and a Cuellar meet but at the only Mexican restaurant/dive bar in the area, right? Good lord, Dad, you could have at least *tried* to have made it a little less stereotypical.

Don't ask me why a mother was out at a dive bar since she had three kids at home to take care of.

Like most machismo, Chicano men of his time, Dad had a soft spot for beautiful women, and to her credit, my mom was a short, little, fair-skinned beauty who looked like Angie Dickenson from "Police Woman." Dad was hooked at first sight.

He had those big-ass, superhero lamb chops on the side of his face—and wouldn't you know it, my mom fell for those things. They soon discovered they shared drinking in common, and were both from southern California. They both liked to smoke, dance together, and drink more together. She already had three kids living in her trailer, but he didn't care. He went to see her every chance he got to party their mukluks off and dance the night away on the sawdust dance floors at bars across Anchorage.

It was all good in da' hood for them, and then *pop!* Two little pink lines, and here I am. They married after I was born then Dad moved into the already cramped, three-bedroom, single-wide trailer.

All the warm bodies did help keep the place warm in the 20-below-zero weather. The water in the toilet would freeze, but with a good-sized poop, it would eventually melt and flush. This is 100 percent true. Peeing in the middle of the night on frozen toilet water, when you're half asleep, wakes you up *real* quick because none of the pee actually makes it in the toilet, and it just splashes *everywhere* like a damn, 4th of July sparkler.

My two alcoholic parents eventually divorced a few years later, leaving Dad heartbroken, with the judge granting my full custody and majority parenting time to what I assume would be his choice of the "least-bad alcoholic parent"—my mother (I'm still pissed at the damn judge. More about that later).

Any young child from alcoholic parents knows how easy it is to distinguish their drunken or hungover darkness from their sober light. It's the smell of their breath and their skin. It's the glassiness of their eyes and the delay in their response and comprehension. Is it a day of slurred speech again—or can they recite the Pledge of Allegiance standing on one leg with one eye open?

When you're a child of an alcoholic parent, you always hope for sobriety throughout the day, but deep down a child's intuition is never wrong, and they already know what the day and the mood are going to bring. It's like living out a day on repeat, with the cycle of crazy playing over and over again. There's a hope, but certainly no expectation that things will be different, or better when living with an alcoholic.

The silver lining was that this experience convinced me that I would never marry a pretty, alcoholic blond, who had no reservations about yelling, screaming, talking over and beating her husband morning, noon, and night. #NeverAgain

At 14 years old, I couldn't take living in that trailer anymore. The lies, the anger, the constant mistrust of people, the frozen toilet bowl water, and the never-ending culture of gossip never resonated with me. The toxicity was something I knew I couldn't have in my life any longer, so I left and moved in with my dad.

Over the years, my mother and I stayed in touch, and she was even at my wedding in 2001. But, I knew I could never fully trust her around my family, especially around my kids. I had to make the decision to remove her from my life, and that broke my dad's heart too. I haven't spoken with her since my oldest son was born, and he's 19 now. My sons have never spoken with the grandmother. Alcohol and divorce just ruin everything.

In 2017, I went through my first (and hopefully *only*) divorce while living in Oregon. When couples with children are divorced in my former county, they are required to attend a state-mandated course, which teaches divorced parents how to interact with one another and with their children during and after the divorce.

It seems like a good idea on paper, but being Alaskan, conservative, stubborn, and Taurus, I didn't take too well to the State telling me what to do, what to say, and how to say it to my children.

I don't know if I have enough pages in this book to write all the expletives my father used when I told him about what the State was forcing me to do.

1. *What the sh**, over!*
2. Oh my achin a**...
3. *You gotta be shi**' me!*
4. *What a bunch of gd horsesh**!*
5. *F-me* (He only let the F-bomb slip out when he really, *really* needed to. It's sort of like "The Power Of Greyskull"—you can only use it when *absolutely necessary.*

I wonder if he said the same thing when the judge told him he had to attend a treatment program before he could see me—every other f'ing weekend. I'm still bitter.

My dad wasn't the only one who was forced to attend treatment classes. After my parents divorced in the early '80s, I was also required to go to counseling as part of an early-intervention program for kids. Yep, seven-year-old me, forced into a "sit-in-a-circle-and-cry-me-a-river" counseling session for kids. I remember thinking how stupid it was then, and 43 years later, it's still stupid now. I guess we don't really ever change the way we're wired.

I absolutely hated the elevator ride to the seventh floor of that building in downtown Anchorage. I still remember it because the classes I had to go to were at night and the building was across from the cemetery, which creeped me out. Even then, I just couldn't figure out what this class was supposed to do for me. It wasn't with our parents, but just all of us kids, the children who were the products of divorce; the real taxpayers of parenting plans.

Week after week, my mother dropped me off to attend another hour-long session, while she went down the street to the Paris Club to have a drink and probably flirt with men. Ironic, huh? There was only *one* reason I actually liked going to those meeting—the cooler full of ice cream sandwiches.

Those are my memories of my "early-treatment" program. The anger, the elevator, the cemetery, the darkness of Alaskan nights in the winter, and the comfort of ice cream sandwiches. But the educated Judge who basked in his own brilliance knew what was best for everyone, I suppose. Damn, I think I need adult therapy to recover from my childhood therapy!

Untreated anger of the past *can and will* fester inside of us, and it eats away any amount of happiness trying to surface in our present state. However, anger can *also* be a trigger to recognize when an unhealthy behavior begins to simmer, allowing us to turn our listening ears inward and turn off the flame before our temper boils over and scalds everyone around us.

It took me a long time, but eventually, I learned how to remove the pot from the stove. It took a divorce, closing a business, moving across the country to Texas, losing my father , and even losing a home. These days it doesn't seem so important to heat my house with boiling water.

The heat of those flames can either harden hearts of clay or soften hearts of wax.

Recently, my oldest boys found this divorce decree dissolving my parents' marriage and started reading it, surprised that I could only see my dad every other weekend. I think now they are starting to understand why I like spending time with them any chance I get. I couldn't imagine seeing them just every other weekend. Life is just to short to live in boiling water.

*I continue this writing about my own anger in story #40, "I'm Still Pissed."

LESSON:

The clanging symbol that is the voice of a loquacious woman can soften even the hardest heart of a district court judge. And as no venom is more poisonous than that from a snake, no anger is worse than the wrath of a drunken and beautiful Latina.

CHAPTER 15

A MEXICANO'S MISTRESS

When my parents were divorced, he took a French class at University of Alaska, Anchorage, so he could impress ladies in the bar. "Cherze la femme" *is the only French he ever taught me.*

Boy oh boy, I could not for the life of me figure out why my dad *loved* Elvira, the mistress of the night on television. As a young kid, I wasn't quite into girls just yet, and I didn't understand what could be so attractive about a goofy woman with a giant wig who never changed her clothes. I just didn't get it. I mean, I *one hundred percent* understand now why he loved her, because, let's face it, the apple doesn't fall *too* far from the tree.

"Dad, why do you like Elvira so much?"

"Because man! She's sexy and I like the curves!"

(Insert internal barf sounds and images here.)

Around that time, I started to learn that Dad had a taste for a certain type of women. When Dad was still single just after the divorce, we'd sometimes go to a restaurant in the winter, The Black Cauldron, in Anchorage, on the second floor of the University Center Mall (in the summer we were too busy fishing). I would eat, and he would just look down from the balcony and watch for pretty women walking below. Like he always said, *"Cherchez la femme!"*

But there was a certain type he always looked for.

"Whoa! Geeze, lady," he'd say. Occasionally I'd just hear a grunt or an "Ooo la la!"

We didn't have any cell phones to keep me occupied, so I had to just . . . watch and learn from the master. The women who caught Dad's eye were a little . . . umm . . . "sturdy," let's just say.

"Dad, why do you like the, you know, the uh, 'sturdy,' ladies?" I asked.

I still remember his look. He was either a little hungover or already a little buzzed, but I recognized that look in his eye and that tongue getting a little thicker.

"I like 'em thick, kid!"

Insert more mental vomiting images, and a strange, internal discomfort in my stomach. Not something a young boy really wants to hear from his dad, and there was no shortage of that type of eye candy for Dad. That was just his thing. No judgement here from me, I just didn't understand his taste in women at the time.

Dad always loved pretty women, and in Alaska, he had a little market niche he carved out for himself. He was a tall, thick, Mexican-American from Los Angeles, with those eternal sideburns of toxic masculinity. He created his own market demand where there weren't any other competitors. Then he made himself scarce, driving up his market value. You've got to work with what you've got and create product scarcity!

Maybe he did sometimes objectify women around me. He was a single, good-looking, Chicano with a good career and lambchops of dreams. I don't blame him, and for reasons found only in the secrets of the universe, women found him attractive. But on the plus side, the apple did't fall too far from the tree!

I'm kidding! I joke! I'm actually very proud of my humility.

This is where I believe the culture of Alaska intersects smoothly with the culture of Mexicanos. Alaskan myself, I know we aren't advocates of the way things are done in the lower 48. We're smart enough and proud enough to figure it out and do it better on our own than they do outside. It's not an arrogance, it's a confidence, hardened by enduring the cold and darkness for years. Reinforced by living in one of the harshest environments in North America. We're fishermen, pilots, loggers, we build 1,100 mile long pipelines, and we are American's military top cover. Once upon a time in the '80s, there was even a world-famous calendar printed called Alaskan Men. There's a mystery and uniqueness about us.

[Enter Mexicanos] It's our way or the highway. We figure everything out on our own and develop the most creative solutions to the most complex problems. We are born with a confidence to succeed, a spirit to work, and a heart to love deeply. Sometimes we have the ego to never throw in the towel, and the arrogance to admire and contemplate our own preeminence. This is why my father fell in love with the place, fit in so perfectly, and called it his home for 50 years. He found a culture which matched his own values, all within the seclusion he was looking for after growing up in Los Angeles.

Me? Like I said, I had already resolved to expand the margins of my existance, and more importantly my appetite. Every child should explore their world and create their own opportunities. I hope I've done that, perhaps with a little of the same spirit as my father, and even my stepmother. Here's to the next phase of exploration! *Cherchez la femme!*

LESSON:

If you're going to objectify women in a shopping mall, don't bring your kid along with you. Not too much wisdom here; just a little common sense. But sense is not always common.

*A funny sidenote: In the '80s we had a country music station in Anchorage, and the program manager apparently told all the DJs that the song 'Elvira' was absolutely forbidden on their airwaves. Not being the conforming type of employee, one brave DJ played Elvira on a random afternoon for all listeners in Anchorage to hear on their drive home from work. As soon as the totalitarian program manager heard the song come through his speakers upstairs in his posh little Anchorage office, he ran downstairs, burst into the studio, ripped the cassette tape out of the player and went straight to commercial.

In an act of defiance, the DJs formed an alliance and all agreed to *only* play Elvira on repeat, hour after hour, day after day, until the program manager issued a public apology! I loved it. After about two days, the PM surrendered and the airwaves were returned to their regularly scheduled broadcasting.

CHAPTER 16

DAD'S DIATRIBES

*O*ne thing about my dad, he said some strange shiz nit.

When I was little, I thought older people said the strangest things. Now that I'm older, I think younger people say the strangest things. Most of the things Boomers used to say make sense to me now, but I need Urban Dictionary to understand some of the things my sons talk about in front of me. On the other hand, they cannot yet fully understand my father's diatribes just as I was unable to. One day they'll be able to understand those timeless sayings and express them with their own children, and I'll continue to do my best researching what in the heck they're talking about! #NoCap, lol!

I have no idea where my dad and his generation of Boomers came up with some of their catchphrases. Many have stuck with me my whole life and have even rubbed off on my kids. I suppose I'm unknowingly passing these down to them because the amount of wisdom and knowledge contained in each one are so unique that they should be recorded for the ages.

A few ground rules of these sayings though: He never said the "F" word in front of me. He had some non-negotiables, and for reasons he took to the grave with him, he never used the 'F' word when I was around.

Not that he *didn't* ever use the "F" word (he did work with GIs for 30 years), he just didn't use it around me, which I have always respected. That's something he passed down to me, and whether it's hypocritical or indifferent, I make it one of my principles to not use the 'F' word around my kids, either. But, give me a little grace if I slip.

He *did* have a strange list of go-to sayings that I think were handed down to most men of his generation from their own parents—The Greatest Generation. But some of these I have *never* heard before, which makes them even funnier and more personal to me.

I think one of the greatest compliments I could ever hope to receive is to hear one of these from some stranger as I'm going about my day in public. For now, they live under my breath in the tiny whispers throughout life, especially since I'm divorced with three boys of my own. I've categorized them as best as I could.

Papa Chuck's Situational Responses of Wisdom and Knowledge:

When it's too cold, outside or inside:

"It's colder than cat shit!"

When it's too hot, outside or inside:

"It's hotter than cat shit!"

When something is too expensive:

"Piss on that horseshit!"

When a politician or car salesman in a cowboy hat at a large dealership in Anchorage comes on the TV:

"Miss on you, pister!"

In times of difficulty:

"Oh my achin ass . . . " (said under the breath, no eye contact, must look down at the floor with hands placed on the hips while shaking head:)

If someone is scared:

"You chickenshit!"

Reading assembly instructions:

"What the shit, over?" IDK if that's a SoCal Mexican thing, or not.

Trying to work on a foreign car from the '80s:

"What kind of Mickey Mouse horseshit is this?"

When the Dodger hit a home run:

"Holy Shitfire, LeRoy!"

When you have to get up off the couch to go pee after hours of watching football:

"Oombagawa!" (If you know, you know.)

When you wake up from a nap and have to stretch:

"Oh me, oh my, oh piss, oh shit, oh dear!" (It has to be yelled at the top of the lungs too.)

Discovering property taxes are increasing:

"Dis is sum buuull chit!"

Finding authentic Mexican food somewhere:

"That's the real McCoy right there!"

Giving 100% effort:

"That's the whole nine yards!"

When something seems impossible:

"Where there's a will, there's a way!" (One of my favorites)

When something is a challenge:

"Let's give it the old college try!" (BTW, Dad. If you're reading this, since I have my bachelors, I give it the old *graduate* try these days."

When his kids, wife, or anyone other than him tries to fix something:

*"Well that's just bassackwards!"**

*I said this a few days ago while my 15- year- old son was in the truck with me. "What did you say dad? Bassackwards? What does bassackwards mean?" It took a minute to register with me. "Wait a second . . . watch your language!" I yelled with a smile.

In times of trouble:

"We in some deep kim chee now!"

Assuming ignorance before malevolence:

"You don't know shit from shinola!"

Sharing an opinion in matters which one has little understanding of:

"You don't know your asshole from a hole in the ground!"

There was a lot of horseshit, catshit, bullshit, chickenshit, apeshit but not *one* "F" word when I was little.

When I called my dad on Sunday nights as an adult, sometimes he would let an F-bomb slip. Not too often, but just enough to still make the sound of it uncomfortable for me all these years later. If you know me well enough, you know I have a potty mouth, but there's not one "F" word in front of my boys. We'll see what happens when they get older and their mistakes get more and more expensive though.

LESSON:

In words and deeds honor your father, that blessings may come to you. And at least try not to use the "F" word so much around your kids.

CHAPTER 17

ATONEMENT

"**D**ad, I need to go to this private school if I'm going to get my life straightened out. Please, I really want to go there."

"Okay kid, let's do it," he said.

My father went to an all-boys' home outside of Los Angeles when he was in his teens, apparently because he was a problem child and "incorrigible," as one of his brothers recently told me. It must be hereditary because the apple didn't fall far from the tree.

I asked him if I could go to a private school after failing the seventh and eighth grade. Technically, I took summer school so I wouldn't repeat seventh grade, but then I failed the eighth grade and didn't want to do summer school again.

Back when I was in junior high and still living in the crumpled beer can of a trailer with my mother, the first week of school started while the US Open tennis tournament was taking place in New York. I loved watching the athleticism of tennis players. I didn't want to go to school because this was well before the time of DVRs, and I would have missed Agassi, Sampras, and most of all, Jennifer Capriati (insert heart bump meme). I skipped my second day of the seventh grade to watch the semi-finals. The next year I skipped the second day of my eighth grade for the same thing. Not only did I love watching tennis, but I also lacked any and all desire t to sit in a classroom in front of a bunch of incredibly unhappy, middle-aged teachers, who loathed their jobs and wanted to make their students' lives absolutely miserable. That's how I felt back then, anyway.

I'm sure my dad felt guilty and partially responsible that his son was following in his footsteps. Man oh man, there was *no* worse student than me. I actually graduated high school with a 1.6 GPA and I am pretty sure I got less than 650 on the SAT. I remember just playing connect the dots when I was filling out the scantron with my #2 pencil.

However, I was lucky enough to have a group of friends in junior high whose family started a Catholic school in Anchorage—Holy Rosary Academy. After visiting there in 1988, I knew I couldn't stay in public schools anymore because they were failing me. A mentor of mine (who happens to be an elementary school principal and someone I highly respect) recently told me, "Chuck, in my 30 years of teaching, one thing I've learned is that kids don't fail school. schools fail kids." I'm not going to argue with him.

At 14 years old I made another decision to leave the frozen tin can trailer and move in with my father across town. Either out of guilt or an effort to "keep up with the Joneses," Dad made the sacrifice to pay the tuition and get me there on time each morning. No more skipping school to watch the US Open.

Mind you, that first year I was at the private school, my dad was still paying my mother $400 a month in child support, and this was in 1988. It wasn't easy, but he had made an obligation to raise his son as best he could. I'm sure his conscience must have taken hold of him, maybe because he felt so incredibly guilty about abandoning his first two children in Los Angeles. If I know my dad, his Catholic conscience began to resonate inside of him, and my tuition was his atonement for abandonment.

Whatever his intention was, Dad, or my stepmom, woke their butts up every damn day to drive me across town to that tiny parochial school with 14 students enrolled, so I could learn about Jesus and keep my ass out of trouble. It worked. The both of them worked the swing shift too and usually wouldn't get home until after midnight. I repeated my eighth grade year at Holy Rosary, then attended ninth grade, before I decided I wanted the experience of a real public high school.

Fast forward 34 years later.

When I flew to Alaska in the early morning of October 18th, 2022 for my dad's funeral, I drove around Anchorage by myself under the same darkness of that sky that watched over me decades ago. It felt like I never left and I could still remembered each street that told a story and each corner that held a memory.

"That's where Floyd used to stand with his sign!"

"There's our old bowling alley!"

"OMG, the trailer is still standing. How is that even possible?"

Funny, I thought I forgot those memories forever. Turns out they were just stored away in my archives.

I looked at one building in particular as I drove through my old stomping grounds, and wouldn't you know it, in the darkness of an Alaskan fall morning, with snow lightly falling from the sky, there was the new, Holy Rosary Academy, 10 times as big as when I'd gone there. What a story of success.

I just stood in the parking lot, taking in the memories of a school and a community that probably saved my life, thinking about the penance my father made for his son, just to have a good education and learn things I've never forgotten, and some things I'll never remember.

I had thought about the people in that school when I had walked across the stage to receive my high school diploma, and later, my college degree. Dad's sacrifice helped shape my own discipline. His atonement sparked my dedication. His penance created my desire to not let fear stop me from doing what's needed for my own three boys.

It sure felt good to make the Dean's list in college, too. It turns out Holy Rosary Academy paid off after all. I'm still a huge tennis fan all these years later too. So are my boys.

LESSON:

Original sin causes a darkening of the intellect. An undisciplined child is an embarrassment to a father. Time has shown me that any discipline we commit to will one day bring immeasurable and unexpected blessings to our lives. And this discipline will most certainly not be easy. Easy holds no value.

CHAPTER 18

ALASKAN VOLCANOS RAIN DOWN

*G*rowing up in the Pacific Ring of Fire was awesome. Back in the '80s and '90s, there were always earthquakes and volcanic eruptions. I seem to remember most of them occurring in the fall and winter for some reason. I mean, how many kids can say they grew up where volcanos erupted and ash fell all over the city? (Pompeii doesn't count. Too soon?)

There are a few active volcanoes near Anchorage, including one across the Kenai Peninsula named Mt. Redoubt. I will never forget seeing the pluming smoke rise up and drift across the sky in person, with feelings of shock, awe, and gratitude. It was an *oye como va* moment.

The Kenai Mountains and the Alaska Mountain Range are part of the Pacific Ring of Fire, a horseshoe-shaped area surrounding the Pacific, with high levels of seismic and volcanic activity. This made things in Anchorage really fun in the '80s and '90s.

Dad called me the night Mt. Redoubt erupted on December 14th, 1989 to make sure everything was okay. He was at work, and I was home alone after school. I didn't even know a volcano had exploded, sending ash into the air for miles in every direction. With my very limited, smooth-brain intelligence, I opened the front door to see what he was talking about. I instantly felt like I had walked into hookah lounge. I took a breath, gagged, choked on the volcanic air, rubbed my eyes, stumbled back inside, and slammed the door behind me.

Learning my lesson not to walk outside during a volcanic eruptions, this time from the safety of our house, I looked through our glass, storm door and could see my entire neighborhood engulfed in a cloud of ash. With the streetlights trying to shine through, I saw little sparkles of volcanic glass slowly falling and covering everything in sight. The ash is *massively* bad for everything mechanical—and for anything that required breathing to stay alive.

Any time a volcano erupted, it took a while for the soot and ash to reach us in Anchorage. With a pluming volcano in the distance, a dark cloud of ash slowly drifts across the sky and stretches for miles. It's basically like a giant cloud of attic insulation floating overhead, which is a great way to keep respiratory therapists busy. It's not like smoke—it's like ash from burned wood but seasoned with microscopic shards of glass.

It was impossible to breathe, and if we went outside, we had to mask up, but even that didn't help very much. The news stations recommended we stay inside until the ash settled, since it destroyed carburetors, motors, scratched glass, and was harmful if inhaled. Surprising as it sounds, 2020 wasn't my first quarantine.

Back then, there wasn't an abundant supply of masks or air filters for cars. Those suckers sold out fast for about three weeks. Nothing ships quickly to Alaska from the lower 48 either, which spiked the demand for masks and filters higher than Mt. McKinley. Honestly, it puffs up the chest a bit when I tell my kids about growing up during earthquakes and volcanic eruptions.

The ash seeped into every nook and cranny imaginable. It really liked to collect on the edge of car windows. Then the volcanic glass scratched *every single car window* when they were rolled up and down.

To my memory, every Alaskan car and truck back then had:

1. Scratched windows and
2. Cracked windshields.

The sight of the ash-covered snow was the worst of all. The ash settled on top of the white snow, turning it into a blackish-brown slush that would later freeze and stay around until spring break up. Then it was washed into the storm drains with the melted snow.

The worst part—we couldn't ride snow machines, dirt bikes, or four-wheelers, and we were stuck inside watching VHS *La Bamba*, and anything else left over on the shelves from Blockbuster.

I remember some people collected the ash and made little statues to sell. Apparently, you can still buy them on Etsy, of course.

Shoot, just a few years ago in 2019, I visited my dad for Thanksgiving. The day after I left, there was a huge earthquake, and the epicenter was directly under his house. Luckily, the same architect that designed Hugh Hefner's bedroom designed my dad's house. Needless to say, it could withstand a beating . . . da dum dum da! (Seriously, that's no BS either, 100% true). Dad let this architect design the house with steel I-beams, sunk 30' into the ground to help make it earthquake-resistant. The earthquake shook plates and bowls out of their cupboards, and left a giant sinkhole right in the middle of the road that lead to his house. It was a "holy shit fire, LeRoy!" moment.

Mt. St. Augustine, Mt. Redoubt, Mt. Spurr, Mt. Illiamna were all active volcanoes while I was growing up in Alaska, and *these* make for excellent roadtrip stories to tell my kid, and even better first-date stories. In the summer of 2024, my boys and I took a family road trip to Estes Park, Colorado, up the Colorado National Forest to the top of the Rockies. After standing outside reminiscing my time growing up in the Pacific Ring Of Fire, I quickly realized I am now a bonefide weather-wimp. I lasted about 30 seconds in the cold, then quickly returned to my truck and turned on my seat and steering wheel warmers. Then, my chest deflated.

LESSON:

Alaska sounds appealing, but don't lift a weight too heavy for you to carry. If you dream of living in The Great Land, be prepared to get your hands dirty, and be on your guard for earthquakes, volcanoes, sinkhole, melting permafrost, black ice, and very high car insurance deductibles.

CHAPTER 19

FROM CHUNKY TO HUNKY

*(O*kay, listen . . . I just thought the title was funny. I'm really not that
egocentric or narcissistic.)

One thing I never did was step foot inside a gym with my dad.

PART 1

I'm a fairly fit, 48 year old (shoot, I'm doing barbell biceps curls
between each paragraph I write to keep the creative blood pump-
ing). My dad wasn't much of a gym guy, so I didn't inherit the fitness gene from him. I did inherit the machismo gene from him
though. He always loved to stay active by going on some adventure
in the north, whether it was snowmachining, fishing, or dall sheep
hunting. He never went to a gym, but it was one of the things he
wanted me to do when I was old enough.

He didn't necessarily want me to be the fittest version of myself when I was younger. If I remember correctly, his exact words were: "I don't want you sitting around the house all day getting fat!"

However, the words were delivered with a chuckle and smile. He didn't necessarily want me to be fit; he just didn't want me to be fat. Well, not any fatter, that is.

Being overweight in our family was *not* okay, and I was constantly reminded of it. In fact, I was the *only* overweight person in my immediate family, and as the youngest, I was a super easy and fluffy target to pick on. These days it's called "fat shaming" and "bullying." Back then it was called, "suck it up, buttercup!"

In our family, it *was* okay to:

Chain smoke

Marathon drink

Grow pot plants at home

Smoke said pot plants

Hide drugs around the trailer

Cuss up a storm

Leave your bong and pipes on the kitchen table

Fight to the death with your spouse or sibling

But you'd better not be fat! You better not!

I mean, look, Dad wasn't wrong. As long as I could remember I was *always* overweight, always the last person picked on the playground, always the slowest (that bugged me the most), and always the chunkiest-monkiest, husky-shopping-section, marshmallow kid in the group.

In fact, that *was* my nickname—"Chunk," and growing up in 1985 did not help with the release of Goonies. I think every one of my friends called me "Chunk," at one point or another. This is around the time I changed my name from Charles to Chuck. Kids were calling me "Chunk," which sounded like my dad's name, so "Chuck" seemed like an obvious right of passage for me.

If we were out on the town, Dad might see an obese person, point to him and say, "See him, kid? That's what you'll look like if you don't stop eating so much!"

I laughed it off. What else could I do?

Ironically, he loved taking me to my favorite pizza joint in Anchorage, Omega Pizza. We'd order a large, black olive and mushroom pizza, and devour most of it ourselves. The best part was eating the cold leftovers on Sunday morning while we watched NFL games from the couch. (Remember, that's why we couldn't go to mass!)

It's not like there was a plethora of fresh vegetables in Alaska, or bougee salad bars downtown. No fresh vegetables or fruit grow there besides some berries, lichen, and tree bark. I do remember having plenty of convenience store burritos, hot dogs, and teriyaki chicken, kept warm beneath the those heating lamps though.

Listen, fat shaming wasn't any funnier back then; it was just more accepted than it is now. I was too short, fat, and too ugly to do anything about it anyway, so I just took it from everyone - friends and family both. We didn't have the cancel culture in the '80s, as we have now, and without social media, people had to say mean shit face-to-face, which I suppose made a person's skin a little thicker. Gen-X has leather skin. Now that I think about it, this totally explains my traumatic triggers when I see black olives and mushrooms on a pizza.

For about the last 20 years, at least once a month, when I spoke with him over the phone on Sunday nights, Dad would *always* ask me, "How much you weigh these days, kid?"

"I'm sitting around 200 pounds of sexy," I'd say.

I could always tell he had a cigarette in his mouth from the sound of his voice, and the shock of me being 5'9" and 200 pounds sent him into cigarette-induced coughing spasms every time.

"Cough! Cough! Choke! Choke! Damn, kid! 200 pounds?" He'd roar. *Cough-gag-cough.* "Sheeeit, you know how much I weigh? 170!"

"Damn, Dad! I got 30 pounds of sexy on you! Good thing you handed down those genes to me!"

In the months before he died, he repeatedly asked me the same questions over and over again. I could tell his memory was fading, but I was sure-as-shit happy enough to answer his same old question and give him the same old answer, just to hear his same old laugh, and cough.

PART 2—HOW DID I GET SO HUSKY?

I'm sure I had a conversation with the Father in heaven before I was born to my parents that went something like this:

"Hey, Charles," The Good Lord said as He was forming me (He still calls me Charles, like my parents did). "What do you want to do when you get down to Earth?"

"Well, Father, I think I want to help others live their best and healthiest life ever. I want to help people discover the strength they didn't even know they had. I want them to be physically and mentally resilient. I want to make people laugh, aaaaaand, *oh!* I want a fun dad too."

"Are you sure?" He said.

"Uh, yeah! What else could I want in life?" I replied.

"Okay, you got it, kid. *Adios! Via con Dios!*"

Then, he kicked me into a run-down trailer park (the same spot Satan must have landed when he was kicked out of heaven), where

I discovered potato chips, ice cream, convenience store burritos, sugar-infused cereal which I sprinkled with more sugar), Maui Wowie, Matanuska ThunderF*** (if you know, you know). Then, he added alcoholic parents and drug-addict siblings. I puffed up like a popcorn kernel on a hot stove. I was the original SWOL.

I served my sentence in that hell-hole of a mouse-infested, frozen-toilet-bowl trailer for 14 years, and when I had enough, I asked my dad if I could live with him instead of my mother. Thankfully, he said yes.

Shortly after I moved in, he purchased a student membership for me to Gold's Gym in Anchorage that spring for $10 a month, because, you know, "I don't want you sitting around the house getting fat!"

As always, he said it with a chuckle to help me remember that he was doing it out of love and not out of spite or disgust.

Nearly every day after school, I took public transportation to Gold's Gym of Anchorage where the owner, Lindsey Knight, would always say, "Hi, Charles!" and welcome me with a smile. I was ready with my yellow walkman, a mix tape of my favorite 1980s big hair bands as I prepped to cower in the corners of the gym and lift quietly by myself, under all my layers of clothes to hide my rolls. It was pretty epic.

Dad always said that I'd never find a girl if I didn't lose my baby fat, and that was all the motivation I needed. *Cherchez la femme*, afterall.

What was my plan to get the ladies? I thought, *"Okay, I'm gonna work my legs every single day. All the regular dudes worked on their beach muscles, but I'll stand out from the crowd and do what they didn't want to—leg day, baby! They got biceps? I got quads!"*

I didn't really know what in the hell I was doing, but I had tree trunk legs already, and after a few years of training I had *ripped, shredded* tree trunks. But my upper body still looked like a wet bag of flour.

Talk about bassackwards! The ladies back then were *not* impressed! I'm *still* trying to dig myself out of that hole too.

If I just lifted weights and went to the gym to go from *chunky to hunky*, I'd be *sure* to land a girlfriend to sit by the fire and chew whale blubber bubble gym with. I'd finally hold a girl's mitten in my mitten and have someone to dogsled with to school in the mornings as we drank warm chaga tea together, watching a volcano erupt in the distance.

PART 3

Skip forward about 15 years, and what started out as a way to burn body fat grew into a habit. That habit grew into a job, and that job grew into a career. In 2003, I became a personal trainer as a side hustle, then in a twist of strange fate, I became a Certified Strength & Conditioning Specialist, opened a personal training studio which later became CrossFit Hilllsboro in 2008. That career allowed me to provide for my family, meet thousands of people who were asking for our help, make a ton of friends, and have a hell of a lot of fun for nearly 20 years.

Dad and Father, thank you both for everything, including all of my struggles growing up that you helped turn into the bedrock for my future.

I didn't inherit a fitness gene from Dad, but he did help me create one. He never got a chance to see the gym I built either. And I'm still trying to fight off the protective layer of Alaskan insulation.

LESSON:

Being poor isn't so bad, but being poor in health is terrible. Nothing is more valuable than health, fitness, and bench pressing your body weight. No happiness is greater than a joyful deadlift, low cholesterol, Fight Gone Bad, and fitting into a great pair of jeans on your birthday. All you have to do do it just take the first step, with the smallest goals in mind. It won't be easy, but just make it simple.

CHAPTER 20

THE ICESPIC

I'm not the whitest Mexican you'll ever meet. That title goes to my middle, red-head child. But I'm a close second.

People often ask why I'm such a white Mexican. When I tell them, "Because, I'm from Alaska," their lightbulb goes off, and they put it together. I can see their wheels spinning and their mouth opens slightly as they figure out the equation.

"Ooooh," they obviously think. "It's cold; there's no sun so he can't get tan. Alaska must be like kryptonite for Mexicans. That's why he's so white!"

Yes, it's true. The lack of sun changed my DNA, and I blend in with the snow to adapt to my environment. I'm like the day walker of Mexicanos. For all that is good and holy, this conversation happens more often than you can possibly imagine.

However, to this day, Mexicanos and Tejanos tend to ask, "Why is your Spanish so good?" Or, "Why do you speak Spanish when you're so white?" (Same as if an American heard someone from Mexico City speaking nearly perfect English.) FYI, I can order food and ask where the library or bathroom is in a nearly perfect Mexican accent. Other than that, don't expect me to have a conversation in Spanish about current geopolitical issues, or ask me to get a Phillips head screwdriver out of the toolbox. I'll just stand there and look at you like an American trying to understand Celsius—clueless.

Half the time most people don't even believe me when I tell them that I'm actually Mexican until I show them my driver's license as proof. My 23andMe test confirms I am 29.9 percent Mexican ("Indigenous") and 57 percent Portuguese and Spanish. But since I was born and raised in Alaska, I'm an Icespic! I have coined this term, and I want a nickel every time anyone says it! My publisher is going to fire me . . .

The next question people inevitably ask is, "How in the hell did a Mexican get up to Alaska?" One person actually figured it out before I even answered. One, and he obviously knew why because we were both in San Antonio at the time—Military City USA. I always filter through my internal bullshit files and choose from a list of answers I've come up with over the years. (I have used all of these at least once):

1. "My parents swam all the way up there."
2. "Dad just kept running north."
3. "Government relocation program: The feds needed to populate Alaska with moose and reindeer herders.
4. Border patrol gave up after chasing my mom and dad when they crossed the Canadian border. They don't always get their man (or woman)."
5. "The CIA offered to put my father in the witness protection program if he worked as an informant against Pablo Escobar. My dad agreed and then the CIA moved us to Alaska to hide.

No Mexican drug lord would ever consider going there to look for him." Yes, someone once believed this story.

6. "My dad was a fighter pilot in Vietnam and the Cold War, and he was stationed in Alaska, flying secret missions over Russia." I used this one in college and some kid believed me for all four years.

7. "My maternal, great-great-great-grandparents, the Cuellars (pronounced quay-yers), migrated from Portugal, over the frozen land bridge that connected Russia to Alaska. The land bridge was also how North America and South America were populated by the people of Asia. Prior to the land bridge melting as a result of global warming shortly after WWI, my grandparents settled in a town near the Yukon Kuskokwim Delta called Bethal, and to this day, some still call it "the white man's village."

Eventually, they made their own village on the tundra and named it Cuellar (Spanish for "The Cold Cellar"—which most people and Google don't know about.) My mother left the village and moved to Anchorage when she was 16.

After the earthquake in 1964, her neighborhood slid into Cook Inlet, which is now called Earthquake Park. Shortly after that, she met my father, Carlos Gonzales who was transferred to Alaska with the Air Force to help rebuild the city after the earthquake.

Since the roads were destroyed, dogsled teams were the only mode of transportation for the next three years. That's also how I got back-and-forth to elementary school, and junior high, eventually being able to ride my snow machine to high school.

My dad loved the seclusion and beauty of Alaska and he stayed up there after rebuilding from the earthquake until the day he died on September 20th, 2022. He spent his final 20 years in the town Wasilla, where Sarah Palin lives, and he could easily see Russia from his house (sans land bridge).

8. And finally, my go-to explanation when I'm asked why I'm so white if I'm Mexican: "Alaskans see the sun only in the months of June, July, August, and part of September. Can you imagine what that does to your complexion? We all looked like those pasty white, skinny jean wearing, glittery, wannabe vampires, but without the sparkles. The lack of sunlight drains the melatonin from our skin, causing all color to fade. I was actually born very dark-skinned, but the lack of sunlight and freezing cold made me look like a vampire in a cryochamber.

This is also how I got my nickname. My closest friends call me "Ice." Not because I'm from Alaska, but because I am the world's northernmost-born Mexican . . . aka, the Icespic.

My mother's parents were very white and actually from Mexico City and Auga Caliente. All of my mother's brothers and sisters and their children are also very white (day walkers). I get my Alaskan complexion from my mother's side.

My biggest, first world complaint is being asked by a customer service agent if I spell my name with a "S" or a "Z."

"With an 'S.'" I reply.

"Okay." They say. G-O-N-S-A-L-E-S?"

Aye caramba...

My favorite example of this cultural inquisition is a salt-of-the-earth, backwoods, good-ole-boy I worked with in Alaska a long time ago. He looked at my last name on my driver's license and thought really hard about how to pronounce it.

"Gone-Zales?"

"Well, that's a new one," I thought.

"Yeah, almost. It's Gonzales." I said.

"What? You're a spic?"

With a side-eyed look of confusion and interest given, I knew I shouldn't hold his ignorance against him.

"That's what I'm told," I replied.

Then it was all good, and we went on our way.

However, let me tell you the worst story about my last name that has both my father and grandfather turning in their graves. This is a 100 percent true story.

I was getting my haircut on Eielson Air Force Base in Fairbanks, Alaska, in 1996. After the barber sat me down in her chair, she looked at me and said, "Are you Italian?" (I get that a lot).

"No, I'm actually Mexican; born here in Alaska though." I answered.

"What? You're Mexican? Wait?" She replied. "What's your last name?"

"Gonzales." I said.

Looking at me intently and thinking as hard as she could, bless her heart, she replied, "Oh, so you're a beaner!" She said with an excitement like she was going to get a discount on landscaping services, or something.

"Uhh . . . well . . ." I stuttered.

The barber in the next stall looked over and said in a thick, Californian, valley girl accent, "Uh, Stacey, I don't think they like to be called that."

"Oh, well, I'm from Southern California and that's what we call Mexicans. It's not derogatory or anything."

Again, this is a 100 percent true story.

I still have no idea what I could have said to a hairdresser, who was standing over me with a pair of scissors. If only Grandpa changed our name to DeNero or something, maybe my hair would not have been butchered that day.

I never met my grandfather, but I suppose he was willing to do anything to grow his business and raise "Americanized" children. This is also why my grandparents never spoke Spanish in front of their children or taught them Spanish, which trickled down to all of us cousins. As it turns out, my mother's parents (originally from Mexico City) did the same thing with their seven children in Santa Barbara, which is why I had to take Spanish in high school and college (got a 'C'), and still have absolutely no idea how to ask what aisle the tortilla chips are on when I'm in a mercado buying ceviche.

I do get complimented quite frequently by the employees on my Spanish when I place an order for two pounds of chorizo and one polo asado chicken. It makes me smile.

"Ju Spaneesh es berry guud!" They say to me.

"Thank you! So is yours!" I always reply. That always gets a chuckle out of them. Always.

I've thought about spelling my last name with a "z" to embrace my culture, but honestly, my kids are so white that would just signal the Armageddon, and they speak Spanish about as well as I do.

At my oldest son's very first check-up, the doctor walked into the room, took a look at us sitting there and with an expression of confusion on her face, doubled checked her chart to make sure she was with the right patients, glanced up at us and asked, "Gabriel . . . Carlos . . . Gonzales?"

"Yes ma'am, that's us. You're in the right room." LOL! I spared her the Icespic Origins story.

I'd feel pretty good about getting a big-ass neck tattoo across my upper back: GONE-ZALEZ! That would get a few laughs out of everyone.

LESSON 1:

The gladness of the heart is the very thing that brings us life and cheerfulness, sometimes mixed with a little BS, always lifts the spirits.

LESSON 2:

Many have fallen by the edge of the scissors of a clueless hairdresser, but not as many as by her tongue.

CHAPTER 21

SMUGGLING CANADIAN WHISKEY

*O*ne thing about my dad . . . he always used to ask me to bring him a beer. One of those cheap, pilsner beers with the little senorita sitting on the moon. I hated it. Every time I brought him a beer I hated handing it to him. I felt like each beer took him farther away from me, farther down a long and dark tunnel, and I was just standing at the other end alone, watching him disappear, slowly becoming smaller in the distance.

To review, some towns are "dry," where no alcohol can be brought in, bought, sold, or consumed. Some towns are "damp" where you *can* import and consume, but not purchase or sell. Some are "wet," because sports bars don't make money in Anchorage off soda and tea.

My dad lived in a "wet borough" called the Matanuska-Susitna, and we could bring it in by cars, trucks, dogsleds or snow machines. It could not be flown in because, on Good Friday of 1964, a bush pilot tried to fly a pallet of stolen Canadian whiskey in to a village. During a violent snowstorm, he crashed the plane into one particular mountaintop of the Chugach Mountain Range in Anchorage. The plane crashed into a cavern and exploded, causing a huge avalanche that wiped out every tree in its path and consequently cleared an area that would later become my high school football field , Robert Service High. The mountain is now called "Flat Top," and it has a hiking trail to the top. It's a nationally registered historic site.

The avalanche opened a pocket of natural gas trapped inside the mountain and *boom!* It blew the top off the mountain and sent boulders the size of a tiny electric car, hurling into downtown Anchorage, destroying entire city blocks of businesses and homes. The boulders landed with such force in West Anchorage that an entire bluff broke away from the mainland and was washed away into the ocean. The event had the force of a 6.4 earthquake, and to this day, the place where the bluff broke away is called Earthquake Park. You can see these images on the internet from the 1964 earthquake.

Even more strangely, the explosion was so strong that it created a shift in gravity in one particular spot on the road leading up to Flat Top Mountain. You can set your car in neutral and can coast *up* the hill. Locals call it, "Gravity Hill." So, alcohol not only ruins everything, it even changes gravity.

Dad often had to wait weeks for his supplies of beer, whiskey, and cigarettes to arrive by 4-wheeler ATVs to the grocery store near his home in Knik. Somehow, he convinced the owner to carry his one brand of cigarettes that I've never seen anyone else in America smoke, Terrytons. I think their old tagline was, "I'd fight anyone for a Terryton." Ummm . . . I don't know how well smokers can fight with a compromised cardiovascular system, so I'm guessing the advertising executive who came up with that campaign is no longer employed by the company.

Be sure to google Earthquake Park, Flat Top Mountain, and Gravity Hill in Anchorage!

LESSON:

Happy are those who have not lost hope. But don't try to find happiness by flying a stolen pallet of Canadian whiskey into Anchorage, or else Middle Earth will open and your only salvation will be a rare tribe of Alaskan Mexicans who don't even live there anymore.

*One of my goals is to turn this book into a TV miniseries. When I imagine this story on the small screen, I think about one person playing the pilot who smuggles the alcohol. I can't state his name, but his ship made the Kessle run in 12 parsecs.

CHAPTER 22

THIRTY MOSTLY TRUE FACTS ABOUT ALASKA

*I*t's my goal after all to put a smile on a million faces.

Here are some random, mostly accurate facts about Alaska and Alaskans.

1. Alaska has no counties. That means there are no sheriffs, either. I still don't really understand the purpose of sheriffs and counties.

2. There are *no* tribal reservations (in all honesty, I'm still not entirely sure what a reservation actually is, exactly).

3. There are no beaches in Alaska. It's all rocky coastline next to *two* freezing oceans (the Arctic and the Pacific) and *three* seas (the Chukchi, Bearing, and Beaufort), on three sides of the state.

4. An ulu (the curved-bottom, Alaskan knife) is traditionally a woman's knife for cutting game.

5. Mosquitoes are the state bird. They can suck up to a quart of blood a day from a caribou, which is one thing that keeps the heard on the move, feeding on the land, controlling vegetation, and limiting the carrying-capacity of the wildlife.

6. The difference between a caribou and a reindeer is that reindeer are slightly shorter, and caribou cannot fly. This is true!

7. There is no state income tax, almost no sales tax, and the state pays you to live there each year, with a check directly deposited into your bank account on October 1st.

8. Alaska only became a state in 1959 and is the 49th state in the union.

9. The 24 hours of daylight means there are 24 hours of photosynthesis, meaning some vegetables get as big as tractor tires. Yes, it's very weird to see.

10. The name Alaska is from the Eskimo word, "Alyaska," which means, The Great Land.

11. The trail for the 1,100-mile Iditarod dog sled race is broken in by snow machines in a race called The Iron Dog.

12. Alaskans call snowmobiles snow machines. But Alaskan-Mexicans call them "snow -ma-cheens!" Yes, we snomacheen with a bottle of tequilla or whiskey in the seat compartment. Anyone who knew my father knows this is true.

13. Parts of Alaska will not see the sun for 60-plus days.

14. Anchorage is the largest land-mass city in the United States.

15. Alaska has no county jails. Since there are no jails, criminals are sentenced to the Alaskan bush (the outer wilderness regions), but they get to choose their location—either the Arctic Ocean or Pacific Ocean coastline regions.

They serve out their sentence by hunting whales, seals, salmon, and caribou, or carving chaga off birch trees for the local Native Alaskan villages.

Because so few people live in Alaska, the lower 48 often sends criminals to serve their sentence in Alaska with work-release programs, and they can choose to stay there after they're released and become a permanent resident, or go back to the lower 48.

16. If you divide Alaska in two, Texas would be the third largest state.

17. If you're new to Alaska, you're a "cheechako." If you're born in or are an experienced Alaskan, you graduate to a "sourdough."

18. We refer to the three major types of salmon as: kings (chinooks), reds (sockeye), and silvers (coho). When you go there to fish, please call the salmon kings, reds, or silvers.

19. If a train or car hits and kills a moose, anyone is free to pack it up and take it home to feed their family.

20. Gas isn't *any* cheaper, even though Alaska produces one-fifth of the gasoline in America. Neither is seafood or ivory any cheaper. By the way, only native Alaskans are allowed to sell ivory to anyone.

21. Ask what an usik is *before* you pick it up with your hands.

22. Alaska has no professional sports teams.

23. The tap water tastes like unicorn.

24. Mt. Denali (formerly Mt. McKinley, which was formerly Mt. Denali) is actually the world's tallest mountain that is *not* on top of a hill, like tiny Everest is.

25. Alaska has no poison ivy or poison oak (that I know of)—which kind of scares me now that I live in Texas and have no clue what it looks like.

26. The only battle fought on US soil during WWII was in Alaska, on the Aleutian Islands.

27. Fifty-two percent of Alaskans are men—which is why I left. (*Not that anything is wrong with that.*)

28. The state was purchased in 1876 for a penny an acre or $7.2 million dollars.

29. You could drive to the state capital if you really, really, really tried. I thought it was nuts when I moved to the lower 48 that anyone could actually go to their state capitol anytime they wanted.

30. For the love of all that is holy, it's pronounced DEN-ALLEY, NOT DEN-ALL-EE!

LESSON:

Set a guard upon my mouth, and a gate at my lips, for I tell the truth according to me! And, we should all try to assume jesting before malevolence (*Credit to Mr. J. Peterson for this lesson).

Left: Lambchops of destiny. I did not inherit his facial hair.

Below:

My first King. 42 inches, 38 pounds. You never forget your first one. Story #2)

My roots, where it all began. The trailer at Top Hand Trailer Court in Spenard, Anchorage. Still standing, more than 50 years later. (Story #1)

AI helped me with this image. I feel like this is what my dad is doing right now.

Above: Fishing, smokes, and I'm sure there's a beer bottle in one of his pockets.

Left: Fishing on the Willow River, in my L.A. Rams jacket. (Story #2)

Above: Snow machining on 7-Mile Lake to watch the re-start of the Iditarod. (Story #11)

Left: It's Floyd!! Honk at Floyd!! (Story #9)

My dad (center), his big brother Richard on the right, and on the left, a family friend who appears in every picture for some reason, Dooley. About 55 years later, Dooley's wife sent me a business card from my grandfather's TV repair shop in Echo Park, Gonzales and Sons. (Story #26)

Original business card from my grandfather's TV repair shop. My dad spend days, and weeks, and years in this shop, learning about electronics, which is how he became an electrician in the Air Force, ending up in the Eagle Keeper Electric Shop on Elmendorf Air Force Base in Anchorage.

Dad flew down for my wedding in 2001, trying to talk me out of getting married. LOL!

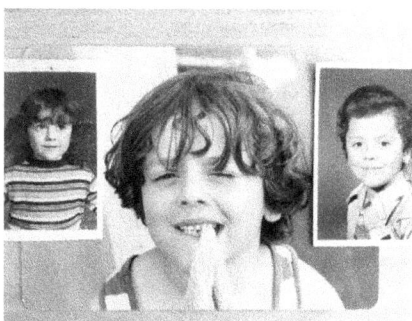

Some early photos of the author.

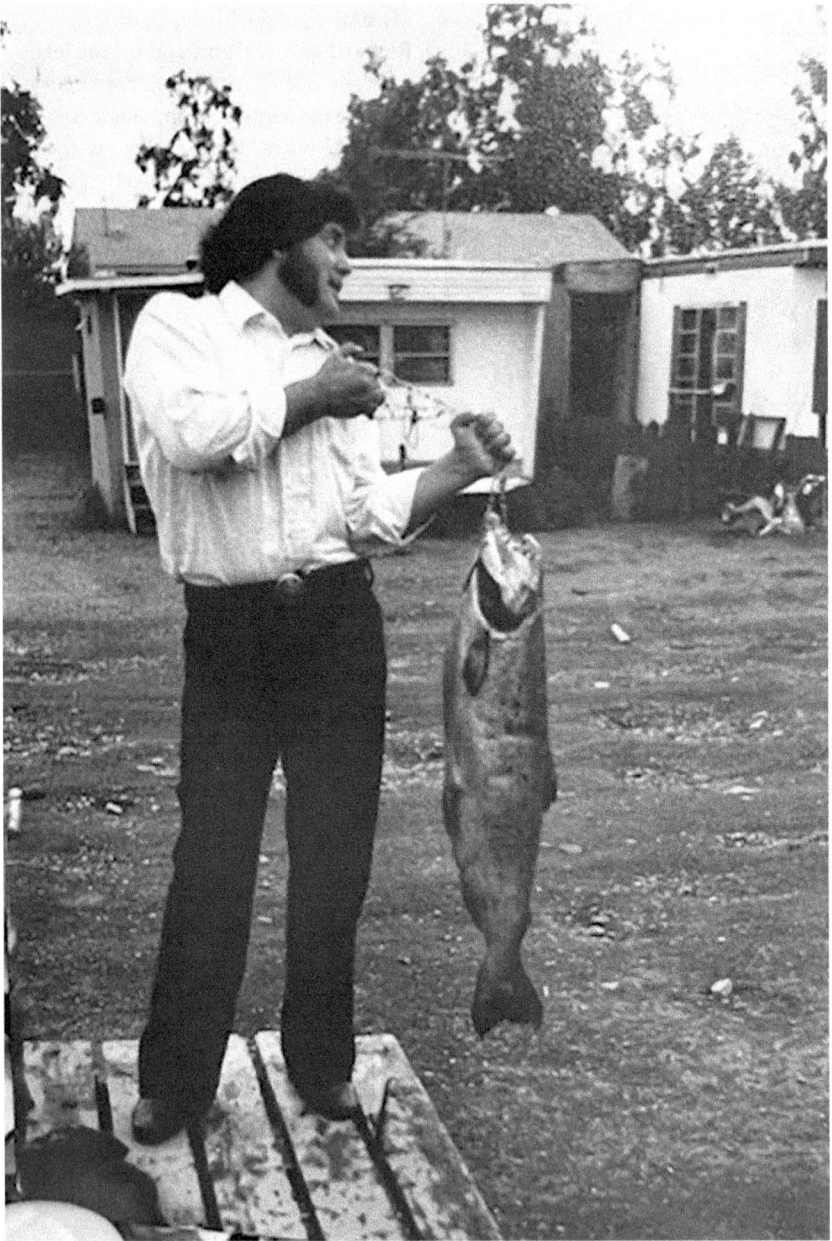

One of the first kings he caught when he was transferred to Alaska.

Dressed up for the Miners and Trappers Ball in Anchorage. At the dinner restaurant, he was actually mistaken as a mariachi for the band.

I briefly tried to use ChatGPT to help me create some photos of my stories. After spending about 2 hours on the instructions and prompts for the first story, I just gave up. But I included it for a funny visual, however inaccurate it may be. (Story #1)

Proud Grandma Mary in front of their home in Echo Park, Los Angeles.

One of Dad's badges. But, he didn't need no stinking badges.

"Beneath those birch trees, nothing could make us afraid, ever." Every once in a while, AI can get it somewhat correct. (Story #2)

Fish on! Not sure where this was in Alaska. Judging from the landscape, cloud cover, and fly rod, I'd say this was on the Kasiloff or Russian River for red salmon in July.

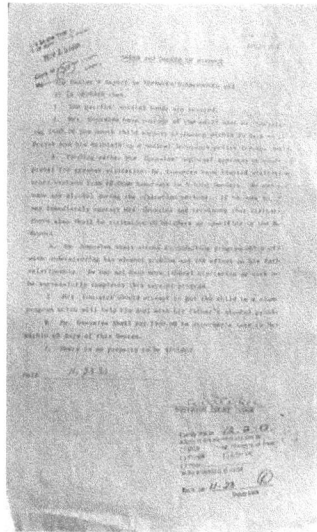

Above: No words needed.

Above right: That damn judges decree. I'm still pissed at Judge Carlson.

Right: Wilma and I saying our goodbyes.

CHAPTER 23

MCCARTHY: AN ALASKAN GHOST TOWN

My dad and my stepmom, Wilma, loved to travel and explore Alaska together. They didn't always tell me where we were going, though and Alaska is a big state to drive around.

During one of the endless summer days in 1992 . . .

"Kid! Pack your shit! We're leaving on a trip," Dad said.

"A trip? Where?" I asked.

"We're driving around Alaska."

"How long will we be gone for?"

"Ten days."

"What? I have to ride in a car with you and Wilma for 10 days? Can I stay home?

"Nope! Pack your shit!"

At the time, that *suuuuucked* for me. I had *absolutely* no idea where we were going. I was just in the back seat, watching endless amounts of trees and mountains pass by while listening to Wilma's Johnny Horton and Engelbert Humperdinck on cassette tapes.

In southeast Alaska, there is a little ghost town that we had never visited before—McCarthy. It's an abandoned copper mining town, next to an ancient path in the earth, carved by a glacier that passed by a few hundred thousand years ago.

How did we get there? We drove 8 hours east on the highway, then 50 miles down a bumpy dirt road going about as fast as a herd of snails running through peanut butter. That road is terrible on bladders, especially for women who have given birth.

Endless dust, potholes, mud puddles, a busted locking hub on the Ram Charger, and I *still* had no idea where we were going!

After our 50-mile trek of bumps and bathroom breaks, the road ended at a rushing, Alaskan river, and a phone booth.

There was no bridge to walk or drive across the glacier-fed, Kennicott River. We had to use the payphone to call whoever was on shift at the bar that night to come down and transport us across in a hand-pulled basket tram, suspended 20 feet over the massive, rushing river. Seriously, I thought we were done for.

The barber/handyman/bartender/mayor was happy to cross the river for what must have been the 10th time for him that day. We hopped in, and this guy pulled the four of us across the river, hand over hand. I still remember how massive this guy's forearms were.

We walked into his bar, and it was everything you'd imagine an Alaskan ghost town bar to look like, including dusty furniture made from wood a hundred years ago. Creaking, spruce plank floorboards and bottles of booze behind the bar looked like they hadn't been dusted in a century. He said we were welcome to walk around town but to *not* go up into the abandoned copper mine.

We definitely went into the copper mine.

When we walked around town on our own, we snuck in the old mine and found the staircase to the top. The wood on the stairs was old and rotting, and each step was followed by creaks and cracks. Besides the sound of debris and rocks falling to the floor beneath us, it was one of the quietest places I've ever been in.

Holes were in the floorboards on every level, and we could see straight through to the rooms below. All of the windows were broken out and, of course, there were no lights anywhere. Dust filled each room, highlighted by rays of sunshine. The view of the Alaskan landscape through any broken window would have taken anyone's breath away.

And, little green rocks were everywhere.

These rocks were the copper they mined back in the 1800s and 1900s. Later, my aunt Betty (Wilma's sister) told me that they were lucky rocks you held to . . . um . . . to . . . let's just say to improve your chances of having conjugal relations. So, as a teenage boy, I stuffed my pockets with those things. Turns out that was a myth.

I still think about that road trip quite a bit, because I love taking fun road trips with my boys these days.

McCarthy is a ghost town intentionally avoiding progress and growth. People came from all across the world to see and experience that nostalgia, and I felt its soul as we walked through that copper mine. I tried to imagine the hardships each of those men and women faced in Alaska over a hundred years ago when they worked in that mine and in that town as I peered out the same broken glass they looked through. The bartender, with his tram-built, muscular forearms and facial hair of a rustic tavern proprietor, the creaking floors, the rays of the sunshine piercing through the broken windows, like angels trying desperately to rescue a soul from the darkness. Listening to the silence has been a part of my soul ever since that day. The last remaining ghost town, built next to the path of an ancient glacier, whispering memories into the imagination to all who wander through its street, sometimes through its mine. Yes, Wilma ignored the 'no trespassing' sign, which made it so much more memorable. To this day, I don't think I would have encroached past that sign.

I don't think we talked too much about that trip. Of course, it was a memorable experience, one which I appreciate now, but at the time I was with two people born in the 1940s, so I didn't have much in common with them as my tour guides. It didn't seem as if I was invited on the trip to build memories with them, I just felt it was forced family time as I was a third wheel in the back. But, to his credit, he was trying to do the right thing, even when he didn't know how to. And that is all that matters, even if I didn't recognize it back then.

Sure, they left me in the car for a few hours while they went into the bar to have some adult time, but I wasn't exactly a peach to be around either since I had an epiphany of wisdom, understanding, and knowledge—the same one my own boys would be blessed with when they turned 14. Though I felt out of place most of the time, just being part of the wagon is what matters most for any child.

Someday, I'd like to go back with my own boys. Maybe I'll show them how to sneak into an old, abandoned copper mine and we can stare out of the same broken windows. I don't think I'll tell them about the legend of the old copper stones though.

Just like my dad didn't tell me.

LESSON:

Happy is the husband of a good wife; the number of his days will be doubled. I guess that means without Wilma, my dad would have kicked the bucket at 38 years old. My father and I would have never gone on adventures like these were it not for Wilma. She was a great wife to my dad and brought the best out of him.

CHAPTER 24

"GONZALES, ARE YOU JEWISH?"

(This is one of my favorite memories.**)** *One thing about my dad, he didn't eat pork. Everyone asked him if he was Jewish.*

At the time, I had absolutely no idea what it meant to be Jewish.

"Dad, why don't you eat bacon?" I asked him when I was about 11 or 12.

"Because, kid, the Bible tells us not to eat pork." I didn't pursue any further questions on the subject after that.

A few years later in 1989, he made friends with one of the best airmen I ever met in Alaska—Frenchie Evans. Frenchie was a black man from outside, who was stationed in Alaska. I loved each time he came over on the weekend because man alive, was he a cultural breath of fresh air.

Frenchie and a few airman buddies came to our house that year to watch the Super Bowl, which was an excuse to drink, eat, and drink.

They all gathered around the *awesome* bar my dad had downstairs—where my high school friends and I *never, never, never ever drank any alcohol down there, at any time. . . .*

Frenchie had brought a few friends over from base to help cook for the Super Bowl and mix some Long Island Iced teas. Dad and I needed the help cooking anyway since Wilma (my stepmom) was away in Arizona visiting family, and we were making pork and beef enchiladas.

So there were three black guys and two of the whitest, Alaskan-Mexicans you've ever seen, throwing enchiladas all over the place in the kitchen, from station to station. Frenchie slapped the tortillas in the sauce, threw them over the counter to dad who added the meat. Dad handed each tortilla to the next guy for the cheese, and I rolled them up, covered them in canned sauce and tossed them in the oven.

That kitchen looked like the aftermath of Hurricane Hugo by the time we were done.

And holy shit fire, LeRoy, if we didn't have that mess cleaned up by the time Wilma got home from Arizona, Dad and I would have been out on our asses selling oranges on the street corner for sure!

"Dad, want a bite?" I had a pork one.

"Nah, kid. You know I don't eat pork."

Frenchie, with a *super* confused look on his face asked my father, "Gonzo, what the hell? You Jewish?" (Gonzo was his shortened nickname.)

"Nah man, the Bible just tells us not to eat pork," Dad replied.

"You do know that's from the Old Testament, right?" Frenchie said. "That's like old shit you don't have to do no more. And you ain't Jewish anyway!"

"Yeah," Dad said

"So let me get this straight, Gonzo," Frenchie pressed. "Out of *all* the things you're not supposed to do from the Old Testament, you're choosing to not eat pork?"

"Yea, man! It says to not eat a split-toed animal. And, all the other shit is fun!" Dad said.

Frenchie broke into tears, he was laughing so hard. "Yea, Gonzo, I don't eat pork either. I'm Muslim."

This is when a *massive disruption of objections* occurred from the other friends he brought over.

"Whoa! Whoa! Whoa! That's some bullshit, Frenchie! I see the booze you drink! You don't go to no mosque! You even smoked last week! That's some bullshit! You a'int Muslim!"

"Hey man, I didn't say I was a practicing Muslim! I'm just Muslim!" Frenchie yelled out.

Back then, Alaska was not known for it ethnic and cultural diversity. It's not exactly the salad bowl as the lower-48 is, which is why I found Frenchie and his friends so funny and fascinating. They just kept drinking and the religious talk was over.

"Hey, Frenchie!" Dad yelled. "Make me one of those Long Island Iced Teas you guys are drinking!" He'd *never* had one before. He was strictly a beer and whiskey guy.

"Hell, yeah, Gonzo. Coming right up!"

After one or two of those, I watched my father standing tall as an oak tree next to the bar, suddenly falling sideways, like a downed spruce tree in the forest, straight down to the floor.

Timber! Bam!

I can still see him falling in my mind, and it still makes me laugh.

"Hey Gonzo, you alright down there? You want one of them pork enchiladas to soak up some of that booze? What about some of this jungle plum?" he asked, holding up a watermelon.

I loved Frenchie. He carried pops up the stairs after that Long Island-Enchilada Super Bowl night.

San Francisco 20, Cincinnati 16.

BONUS!

Hey, Frenchie! In 2023, I sent in my DNA for analysis, and wouldn't you know it, I'm 1.5 percent *Ashkenazi Jewish!* We *are* Jewish after all, Frenchie, *L'Chaim!*

LESSON:

Fun during a Super Bowl is fine, but if passion is always satisfied, eventually someone you work with will carry your ass upstairs to put you to bed, and that's just embarrassing, forever.

We're still trying to watch Cinci win a Super Bowl, too, some 34 years later.

CHAPTER 25

MATCHING SCARS

One thing about me, my dad, and my first son, Gabriel, we all have matching scars on our noses.

My dad had a scar right at the bridge of his nose. When I was about 10 years old, I asked him how he got it.

"That damn cockatoo (our pet bird), Oscar! He bit me!"

When my oldest, Gabriel, turned 10, he was playing with our little dog, Carter. Carter was a Lhasa Apso and would sometimes get nippy if you got too close. Wouldn't you know it, Gabriel got too close one day and got nipped right at the bridge of his nose. Now Gabe has a scar.

When my middle, redheaded-ginger-Mexican, Gavin, was about eight, all of us went swimming one afternoon. I thought doing a backflip while standing in the four-foot-deep kiddy pool was a feasible idea. I jumped up, flipped backward and *bam!* Scraped the bridge of my nose on the pool floor. Bleed, bleed, bleed everywhere. Ouch.

My dad, Gabriel, and I all have scars across the bridge of our noses. But the story doesn't end there. . . .

Sometime around 2015, I mentioned to my dad how I scraped up my nose in the kiddy pool.

"Dad, remember when Oscar bit you and gave you that scar?"

"What the hell are you talking about, kid?"

"When our cockatoo bit you and gave you that scar on your nose?"

After a long, thoughtful pause he broke into laughter. "*Ha!* That bird never bit me! I got in a car wreck in Anchorage. My nose hit the steering wheel, and I didn't want to tell you! Sheeeet, I forgot all about that!"

*Make a mental note of this car accident to reference a story later in this book.

Mic drop. Jaw drop. Some 38 years later, the truth was finally revealed. Now I'm just waiting for my two other sons, Gavin and Max to make their own bad decisions—which will result in a great story about how they got their own nose scars. We Gonzales men are good at three things:

1. Making bad decisions
2. Telling great stories
3. Pissing off the women we love

LESSON:

In my youth, I was blinded by my own inexperience. In my 48 years, I am now blinded by what I think I know. As much as we think we know those who are closest to us, we may never know their real stories. We don't know what we don't know, and I wonder what I won't know tomorrow.

What I do know is bad decision make good scars and great stories.

CHAPTER 26

A KNOCK AT THE DOOR

"**M**rs. Gomez, I'm sorry to have to tell you this, but your husband has been killed in action overseas in the war."

*I wish I knew more details about this story.

Dad came from a very big family of Gonzaleses in SoCal, but he also had two older brothers, Richard and Bobby Gomez. They shared the same mother, Mary, but Richard and Bobby were from their mother's first marriage to a soldier in the U.S. Army named Frank Gomez.

Frank met my Grandma Mary in Colorado sometime in the 1930s, before the U.S. officially entered WWII. Frank was already in the military when he met Mary, and shortly afterward they were married and moved to Los Angeles.

A few years later, he received his orders to ship off to Europe to serve his country in WWII. About six months into his deployment, my grandmother, his wife, heard a knock at her front door. It was a military chaplain, bringing the news that no wife should ever hear.

"Mrs. Gomez, I'm sorry to tell you, but your husband was killed in action."

I can only imagine how she took the news of becoming a widow, with little Bobby and Richard to take care of all by herself in Los Angeles. The tears for her two sons growing up without a father must have salted the floor of their home and the beds they slept in that night.

She did her best to survive on her own with her two sons, but she knew they needed a father, and a little more than a year later, she met another man—my grandfather, Polo (Paul) Gonzalez. They didn't waste any time having children, and her baby-making factory kicked into high gear, bringing ocho (eight) Chicanos into the world. My father, Carlos, was the firstborn of the *Gonzales* kids.

But wait, the drama continues.

Fast forward another year, and there's another knock on the door.

Knock, knock, knock. Who could it be at the door, you ask? You guessed it. Frank Gomez was standing at the front door, dressed in his military uniform.

This is where you'd insert one of my dad's catchphrases:*

- Holy shit fire, LeRoy!
- Oh my achin' ass...
- You gotta be shitting me!
- What the shit, over!
- *Oh me, oh my, oh piss, oh shit, oh dear!*

*Now that I think about it, I bet my dad got each one of those catchphrases from his mother, at that exact moment, and they stuck with him forever.

The Army had made a monumental mistake. Frank was *missing in action* and not *killed in action*. When he was found, he was ordered to head back stateside to be with his family.

Frank must have been prepared for what was about to happen. He must have known that she needed to move on without him, after she was told he was K.I.A. I can't imagine how shocking that must have been for her, or how painful it was for him.

Paul was home, too, and I sure as shit know he wasn't prepared for it either.

My uncle Richard, the oldest of the Gomez boys recently told me that Frank and Paul went toe to toe right there at the entryway of the house in Echo Park. I don't really blame either of them.

I can only imagine the play-by-play that afternoon. My grandfather wasn't a small man, and from what my father told me, I inherited his "barrel-chest." I wonder if Grandma threw her slippers at them both. At the end of the day, uh, rather, at the end of the fight, Frank knew he had to move on. Apparently Granda' Paul's pecs prevailed.

Frank went back to Colorado, and Grandma chose to stay in L.A. with Paul and raise all of her children together in one house. "Conjuntos." They lived in that little home for decades, complete with an avocado and lemon tree.

Polo Gonzalez became the first entrepreneur in my father's family. He opened a television repair shop in Los Angeles, "Gonzales And Sons," and made a career out of it. *Polo Gonzalez* later changed his name to Paul Gonzales, which is why we all spell our last name with an 's' instead of a 'z' and it still drives me crazy. Here's why.

During that period in America, many U.S. born, Mexican-American Chicanos felt their children needed to become "Americanized" to fit in, so they changed the spelling of their names. If you have the old VHS of *La Bamba*, remember Ritchie Valens was really Ritchie Valenzuela. I'm not too sure how "Gonzales" is more America than "Gonzalez." Maybe "Smith," or "Washington," or Johnson" would have really tipped the scales?

"Oh, you're brown, you speak English, and you spell Gonzales with an 's'? You MUST be American! Here, fix my TV, and take my money!" Not really sure if there was the metric Grandpa used to increase the number of customer leads based on changing a consonant in our last name. As I said, I don't blame him.

I wish I would have met my Grandpa Paul. I can tell my father looked like him, and people used to tell me I was the spitting image of my dad. Grandpa had a barrel chest, became a businessman, had a fighting spirit, and taught my father how to make things figure-outable. I hope he knows how much of him has been passed down.

For the record, my mother's father, Joseph Cuellar, was a boxer, a banjo and guitar player, and an entrepreneur, as owner of Cuellar Pastries in Santa Barbara. It's just in my blood, and my blood sugar. I never met either of my grandfathers.

LESSON:

A blow from a Latina's sandal raises welts. But a blow from the tongue of an Army Chaplain will break hearts, and the blows of an angry husband will break bones. And I choose to never raise my children in such seclusion away from their family, which is one reason I don't live in Alaska anymore.

CHAPTER 27

THE MERETRICIOUS-MACHISMO MEXICANOS

"*D*ad, *if you were an animal, you'd be a rizzley bear.*
If you did magic, you'd be the Rizzard Of Oz.
If you had a bomb, you'd be a domestic terrorizz.
If you played ball, you'd be a Memphis Rizzley."
—My second son, Gavin. 2022

*For the older generation, here's the definition for RIZZ: *Another word for spittin' game/picking up ladies.*

Person 1: Are you from Tennessee , because you're the only ten I see."

It's 1985 and my father and I are prepping ourselves with hairspray and cologne to hit the town on Saturday afternoon.

"Damn, I'm good-looking, kid," he said as we both stood in front of the bathroom mirror in his apartment, getting ready to hit the arcades for my weekend of video games, pizza, and *cherchez la femme* with him.

"Yep, it must be in the genes!" I agreed as I stood next to him, while we were contemplating our own awesomeness. (Narcissus did the same thing while looking at himself in the reflection of the lake). I was experiencing the trickle-down effect of the Gonzales Macho Complex (GMC), which evolved into the patrician of the trailer park.

We were so full of the shit, mister.

In the Mexican culture, there's something called "Machismo," or as most women call it, *"pinche* machismo!" Or, meretricious-*machismo-Mexicanos!*

Machismo is described as a strong or inflated sense of traditional/ toxic masculinity placed on physical courage, virility, often accompanied by a sense of grandeur." Funny—"magnamic" and "grandeur" are two words in our family crest.

Yep, that pretty much sums us up.

But that damn inflated ego complex does nothing more than bring trouble to your doorstep every turn. The bad thing is it tends to be handed down generationally. *Luckily,* I was fat and out of shape, with big, curly hair and acne, so I didn't have too much to be machismo about when I was younger, thank God. Maybe that was part of His plan too.

Dad always took pride in how he and I should look in public. When my parents were still married, he used to dress me up in a suit and tie when we went to the movies. I don't have many memories of them together since I was so young when they divorced, but dressing up for the movies and Easter pictures are some of them.

Years later, I asked him, "Dad, why did you always dress me up when we went to the movies?

"Because I didn't want you looking like shit when we went out anywhere!" (As a father of three boys, I can completely understand.

I ain't tryna dress up my boys when we go to the movies though. Let's just get everyone out the door on time and call it a win.)

Contrary to his likely belief, Dad wasn't the most handsome of his brothers, but that didn't stop him from thinking he wore the crown. That title went to his brother, my Uncle Gilbert Gonzales. Gilbert was the lady's man. He was the Charming Chicano, The Rizzler of Echo Park, the most handsome of the Gonzales and Gomez tribe (so I'm told), and my dad's little brother.

Grandma Mary had really good-looking boys, all believing they were the best-looking of the bunch. For the life of me, I just couldn't understand how any woman found my father attractive. He had those damn lamb-chops-of-destiny and that combed-back, Mexican-afro full of hairspray, with a beer belly, and driving a yellow low rider. Maybe that was just how a player played in Alaska back in the '80s. Don't hate the player. Hate the game!

Gilbert grew up with the rest of the family in Echo Park, an upper-lower-class neighborhood back in the '50s & and '60s, and had all the RIZZ. They were the traditional, white t-shirt, khaki pants, dress shoes, and spit-shined cars kind of Mexican-Americans, who didn't speak a lick of Spanish, as to be "Americanized" and accepted. Most of their kids (my cousins) don't speak too much Spanish either.

All nine of them lived together in a tiny house, with a lemon tree and an avocado tree in the backyard, which is why my dad, and so many Los Angeles-born Mexicans, can sink their teeth right into a lemon without giving it a second thought. No different than an Alaskan walking barefoot in the wintertime outside to catch the dogsled team bringing the monthly mail. We're all just products of our environments.

My father followed in the footsteps of his older brother, Richard, and joined the military. He signed up with the Air Force right around 1966 and was shipped off to Greenland. After a few years, Dad let the family know he'd be in town for a few days to visit them. Gilbert became a little anxious and had a conversation with his big brother Richard.

"Richard, I have to join the Army like you and Charlie did."

"Why in the hell would you want to do that?" Uncle Richard asked.

"Because, I don't want Charlie to be disappointed in me when he comes back, and I don't have my shit together yet. You joined, he joined, now I have to do something."

My father never heard one word of this story when he was alive. It would have crushed him forever for what was about to happen to his little brother.

When Gilbert left Los Angeles, that was the last time my family ever saw the real Gilbert.

Gilbert, the most handsome of the sons, came back as an experimentally medicated, drugged-up test-bunny from the Army. Uncle Sam decided they needed his body and his brain for experimental treatments, and instead of coming back with superpowers or adamantium claws that shot out of his fists, he came back barely being able to mentally function.

It broke my family's heart—especially my dad's since he was the big, overprotective brother. Still, Dad never knew why Gilbert had actually joined the Army in the first place.

Gilbert lived out his days on the streets of L.A., visiting family members from time to time. I only met him twice when I was younger. When I saw him, his hair and beard had grown out for months, and he was dressed completely in rags, his shoes held together with a few pieces of string. I just thought he was the crazy uncle (we all have at least one), and Gilbert didn't really resonate with me. But his mother, brothers and sisters loved him dearly.

But wait, there's more...

Yes, there exists another mysterious-meretricious-machismo-Mexicano uncle who was so taken with himself, and who contemplated his own beauty for so long that his mind drowned in his own grandeur.

Uncle R., let's call him, the youngest of the Gonzales children, was certain his father was John F. Kennedy and his mother was Marilyn Monroe. I shit you not.

You can't make this stuff up—I have two brothers named Raymond, an uncle who was chemically experimented on by the military, another uncle who thinks he's the love child of JFK and Marilyn, *and a* dad who thought he was the spitting image of a Mexican Elvis. *O-em-gee!*

In case you're wondering, Uncle R. doesn't look anything like JFK or Marilyn. He looks just like his other brothers and sisters.

Let me tell you, in all honesty, those are very difficult cords to cut—those machismo, egocentric, masculine, testosterone-driven, generational power chords of pride and dominance. It's why I pray so hard over my boys for confidence powered by humility and ambition powered by compassion.

As it turns out, my boys think the same thing about me as I do about my machismo uncle and dad growing up in Echo park. Nay, though I cannot grow the lambchops-of-love on my cheeks, nor possess the valiant *machismo low rider*, I can play point guard with my dad and uncle on the Memphis Rizzlies.

I know, it's a sickness we have.

LESSON:

Later in his life, it was easy to judge Gilbert with our own righteousness, but that's just an alternate route to amplify our own sin, one which we inevitably causes us to fall on our own sword. Ain't nothing wrong with givin' ourselves the esteem we deserve. But, for Pete's sake, have a little serving of humility with that entre of ego.

CHAPTER 28

ONE IS ONE
TOO MANY...

One thing about my dad he drank some nasty booze. Yuck.

As the youngest child of alcoholic parents, I had to learn from the mistakes of my family that, at the end of the day, cheap alcohol just isn't worth the headaches and hangovers the next morning. In my self-guided studies of being a child of alcoholic parents, I also learned that their youngest children are often the most creative — typically because we're always looking for discreet places to hide from them. We also have to hide anything of value from them so they won't steal and sell it to one of their friends or a pawn shop. We have to find the paths of least resistance away from them because any spark could cause a nuclear chain reaction of endless, unforgiving anger.

Action: You walk too closely to them.

Reaction: "What the F is your problem? Get your fat ass in your room."

Action: You look at them the wrong way. Maybe a look of resistance to their authority:

Reaction: "You got an f'ing problem? What, you think you're better than me?"

Luckily, my father was not a mean kind of drunk. My mother and some siblings on the other hand—Lord, just thinking about it makes the systolic blood pressure jump.

The other night I walked into a liquor store and lo and behold: There on the bottom shelf, a lone bottle caught my eye. Just a little sign from my Pops that he's either:

1. Dying for a drink or
2. Telling me to stay away from Scotch.

I had no idea they still made Cutty Sark, and I haven't seen it for nearly 40 years. It was my dad's original nightcap back in the '70s, and I still remember the one-gallon, green bottle, pivoting in it's wooden cradle.

The lone Cutty Sark bottle turned into a coin jar, on top of the green, immortal, frost-growing refrigerator that rattled all damn day and night. Later, Dad accidentally shot that refrigerator while cleaning a handgun, and it still didn't die!

What was it about our parents' generation and hard alcohol? It seemed like the harder they worked, or maybe the older they got, the stiffer their drinks. And the more they drank, the more they smelled of alcohol—especially the next morning. The "alcoholic's aroma" instantly reminds me of the darkness and evils of addiction.

Sometimes I'll meet a person with this same smell—usually a car mechanic or an old electrician—with alcohol and cigarette stains on the bottom of their white mustache. It always stuns me for a moment, and the trigger takes me on a ride through memory lane as I instantly pass by visions of cigarette butts in dirty ashtrays and empty beer bottles. Funny how smells can unearth what is buried deepest.

Even as a child of alcoholic parents, more specifically, as the youngest child of alcoholic parents, I still don't understand alcoholism. I understand the effects of it quite well, but I don't understand it as a vice that can control a person's desires and impulses. Ask any Alaskan, and he or she will tell you that Alaska has more alcoholics per capita than anywhere else in America. Ask any Mexican and they'll tell you that 90% of their aunt and uncles, 75% of their cousins and 50% of their brothers and sisters are alcoholics. I've never come across that study or any evidence that supports the claim, but I imagine it's 10% margin of error.

Sometimes people just deal with the darkness, isolation, the cold, cabin fever, or even the endless hours of sunlight better with alcohol. It doesn't help them "deal with" or solve anything. As far as I can tell, it just makes them marinate in and worry about their own life and the problems of the world even more than they did when they were sober. A perceived solution which advertises the destination of greener, happier pastures, but after derailing, it only leads to more destruction, never letting the traveler arrive where they intended to go.

FYI: No matter what it takes, no matter the cost, for the love of all that is good and holy, never talk politics with an alcoholic, Dad *needlessly* worried all the damn time about the US going into war, the global supply chain, and the price of tea in China on Tuesday. "Sure, Dad. You *absolutely* know what's best for everyone in the country right now with Gorbachev and Regan at each other's throats. In the early 1980s, when mountain bikes first entered the market and became popular, he took me down to REI sporting goods in Anchorage, so we could look at them.

"Dad, why do you want to look at mountain bikes?" I asked.

"Because, kid, I think we might go to war with Iran or one of those countries, and if we get bombed or can't get gas for our cars, we'll need mountain bikes for transportation. "

I think this was the first time my dad's sayings started their journey from the ether of the universe, through my brain, and out my mouth with a whisper.

"Oh my achin a**?" I said under my breath.

"What did you say?" He replied.

"Uh, I said, *where are we going to eat?*"

He looked suspiciously at me and smiled, "Kid, why are you always thinking about food?"

We never bought mountain bikes—he was too cheap and those suckers were expensive in Alaska. Plus, he was still shelling out $400/month in child support, and I already had a Redline BMX bike, so I was good. But he was *always, always* worried about the US military strategy until the day he died. He was a perpetual worry-wort.

"*Oh, shit,* we need to bomb those sons-a-bitches," he'd say. "Damnit, now we're going to war, and we need to move out into the sticks so we can take care of ourselves! And kid, *do not let your boys join the military, damn it!* This president doesn't know his a**hole from a hole in the ground!" He said that about every President. It just becomes endless, day after day, night after night. Thankfully, I've stopped watching the news and Sunday night, televised news magazine years ago. With three machismo-Mexicanos of my own to watch over, I have more important things to worry about like, how many books do I need to sell for a dozen chicken eggs?

LESSON:

Alcohol drives a stake between the fitted stones of family, and the fruit of the tree shows the care it has had. Care for your best fruits first, because one day you're going to wake up and they'll be gone, tending to their own garden, protected by their own stones they've placed. I hope my own sons will set my stone upon their wall, and not kept outside in an empty field.

CHAPTER 29

LISTEN TO THE PHYSICIAN

O*ne thing about my dad, he hated doctors.*

He also *hated:*

- Doctor appointments
- Traffic
- *All* drivers
- Most people who were not family or military
- Flying
- Any and all rules
- Being told what to do
- Answering to anyone
- Customer service reps
- The heat (I mean the weather, not the police)
- Mexican food in Alaska
- Gyms
- Healthy food

- Shopping malls
- And stop lights

Remember the story about our nose scars? Well, when he got into that car wreck in 1981, he also injured his hip pretty badly. Because he hated spending his money on doctors , he never scheduled an appointment to have it looked at. It bothered him for *decades*, but he'd still always yell, "doctors don't know shit from shinola anyway!"

When he was about 65, he couldn't take the hip pain anymore and finally decided to do something about it. His wife, Wilma, scheduled an appointment with a specialist, and afterward, the doctor recommended a hip replacement—to which my father reluctantly agreed.

After the surgery, the doctor had a little conversation with my father.

"Okay, Mr. Gonzales, your wife tells me that you're quite the drinker and smoker. Is that right?"

"That's right, doc. Ever since I was 15 goddamn years old."

Maintaining a professional composure, he took a deep breath and did his best to describe the risks of drinking post-surgery to a life-long alcoholic and smoker. "So, let me tell you what's going to happen, Mr. Gonzales. If you go home and start drinking and smoking after this surgery, you'll get a nasty infection in this hip joint, and it will hurt like hell, get infected and ooze pus all over. If that infection gets to the new steel I just put in your hip, you'll need your leg amputated. Got it?"

"Suuuuuuure, doc. Riiiiight. I got it." He said as sarcastically as humanly possible.

That stubborn, damn Mexican-Boomer went back home and started drinking and smoking as soon as he sat his ass down on the couch. Doctors . . . what do they know after only 16 years of schooling, right?

Of course it became infected and hurt him like hell. It oozed pus and turned green and all sorts of colors. He had to change his bandages regularly throughout the day, and he couldn't walk because it hurt too much. He was in some deep kimchi, and all of us were afraid he'd need an amputation.

After a few weeks of moaning, groaning and being a complete pain in the butt to those closest to him, he couldn't take the pain anymore and mustered up the humility to call the doctor and tell him what had happened. He landed back up in the hospital, and his conversation with the doctor was priceless.

"Hey! Mister Gonzales! I'm so glad you're here and I see you followed my orders to a 'T'. Well done!" The doctor said. "Let me tell you what's going to happen now. I've spoken with your wife, and I'm putting you in our in-house care unit for 10-days, and you will have *no* access to alcohol or those got-awful cigarettes. Now, I need to take a look at your infection and see if it reached the steel. If it did, we'll have no choice but to amputate your leg. Got it?"

The doctor came back with the test results and thankfully, the infection did *not* reach the steel. Eventually, Dad went home with as many legs as he went into the hospital with, but the bad news for him was he couldn't drink or smoke for a month, and he had no choice but to kick two bad habits overnight.

For the first time in 50 years, my dad was sober, and it was amazing to hear the clarity in his voice and mind again whenever I called to check up on him. It was such a refreshing change from the buzzed, thick-tongued, and often immature voice that was usually on the other end of the phone when I called on Sundays. If I'm being honest, I never thought of my dad as an alcoholic, I just thought of him as someone who lived by breathing oxygen and drinking beer. To me, it just seemed normal to have a dad who loved his "whiskey, beer, cigarettes," as he would always say. It was a shock for me, and I'm sure for everyone else too, to see my father live in a world of sobriety.

His spirit seemed clear, too. I thought about how he might be able to start traveling again, go camping and fishing again, and maybe even come down to the lower-48 and visit us. The 10-days went by quickly in the hospital and after he was released, he even stayed sober once he went home. But the hopes of long-term sobriety were short-lived for all of us, and after about 90-days, he could no longer break free from those old habit. He loved his trifecta of demons and he wanted to live his life and go out on his own terms.

I'm not sure if he ever got the chance to go fishing again after the surgery, I don't believe so, and that was always his favorite thing to do during the endless summer days in Alaska: fishing on the banks of a river in hip waders, a beer in his hands, a thermos of black coffee, Tareyton hanging out of his mouth, and another beer tucked away in his green, camo rain jacket (hidden from those peskey fish and wildlife officers).

Dad wasn't able to do quite a few things in the last few years, but to his credit, he lived his life how he wanted, and he left this world on his own terms: Lying on his own couch, in front of his huge living room windows "25 miles from no where," and asleep on the edge of the Alaskan wilderness.

LESSON:

A furnace may test the work of the smith, but beer and Tareytons will test the patience of an orthopedic surgeon. And, for the love of all that is holy, if I ever think I'm the smartest one in a room full of doctors and nurses, please just hit me over the head with a bottle of sparkling water.

CHAPTER 30

EVERYTHING IS FIGUREOUTABLE

One thing about my dad, he didn't just talk about doing things, he did all the things. He figured it out for himself.

Many of my dad's eloquent catch phrases (chapter 16) pop up for me when I stub my toe, or get a collection letter from an unpaid parking ticket. But more than a man of words and sayings, he was a man of doing—a man of action and follow-through. He was one of those dads from the '80s who could fix anything he touched; someone I held the flashlight for.

He never had the fear of starting an adventure. No, that's not actually correct. Rather, he never let fear keep him from starting an adventure. Neither was he afraid to tackle a project and find a way to figure out a problem. #FIGUREOUTABLE.

In Alaska during the '70s and '80s, you had no choice but to figure out how to survive the freezing cold and the dark, especially when you live in a single-wide trailer, built in the '60s. Remember, as I mentioned before, to give you an idea of how cold trailers get in Alaska, we would shovel snow against the trailer to help insulate it from the cold. That didn't work too well when most of the windows were either cracked or broken. To warm up, we quickly learned to open the door of the laundry dryer, place a piece of duct tape over the door sensor, and turn the knob to 'on' while standing in front of the machine with a large blanket draped over us to trap in the heat and warm us up, for a while. #FIGUREOUTABLE

Then we'd accidentally go pee in the toilet bowl with frozen water.

I mean, this guy, straight out of the streets of Los Angeles figured out how to:

- Set up camp and pitch a tent in the Alaskan wilderness
- Cure salmon eggs to use a bait on Spin-N-Glo lures for king salmon
- Go Dall Sheep hunting in the Chugach Mountain Range
- Repair anything on vehicles
- Replace a joystick on an F-15 fighter plane
- Build a fire in the wilderness
- Teach his kid how to change the oil in his vehicle, and change his own tire
- Load up and go snowmachining for the weekend
- Make his own bullets and hit a target 300 yards away with a 30-06
- Build an entire house "25-miles from nowhere," as he would say
- Drink a fifth of liquor, a six-pack of beer and smoke a carton of hideous cigs each week for almost six decades.
- And . . . how to leave this world peacefully, in his sleep

He was so damned stubborn and pigheaded, he just put his head down and figured out his own solution. To him, everything was *figureoutable*.

"Where there's a will, there's a way!" he'd say.

"Let's give it the old college try!" he'd yell with excitement.

He wasn't necessarily excited about figuring everything out, nor was he the most patient person in the world. In fact his figureoutable projects always involved his frequent catchphrases in a guttural yell from his diaphram. (Funny, at this moment my 16-year-old is working on my truck and just yelled out in frustration. He's figuring it out, but his voice sounded just like Papa Chuck's, which made me smile. And as God as my witness, he came into the house and said, "Dad, I figured it out").

I have to admit, each time I fixed anything in our trailer, my home, or in my business, I thought about my dad and hoped I'd be able to fix it as well as he did. I never spent the time to figure out one of his favorite toys, a voltometer. I always got stuck on the *"why and how?"* settings in my brain.

Even more impressive, Dad made his dreams happen in Alaska, where just about everything is (or was back then) a gigantic pain in the ass. It's dark. It's cold. It's in the middle of nowhere, and you have to wait weeks for anything to be shipped in from the Lower 48. But he never let that stop him from having a hell of a time and figuring it out.

One winter weekend, he decided to take me skiing on a bunny hill on base. Can you imagine that? Two Mexicans skiing on a bunny hill in Alaska with *absolutely no idea* what we were doing? After we rented our skis, I looked at the rope tow and was terrified. No way would I be able to hold onto that thing all the way up the hill. But I'd "give it the ol' college try," as my old man would say.

We had no idea what we were doing, but he figured it out.

Leave it to the Air Force to station a Mexican from Los Angeles in Anchorage *and* in Greenland! Seriously, you can't make this stuff up. I'm sure he must be the last Alaskan Mexican to serve in Alaska *and* Greenland.

Greenland is where he started to realize it was possible to create his own future, and that he didn't have to "lose his identity" (as he would often say) by living in a big city. He figured out that he could make a new life and create his own opportunity outside of the big cities. His eyes filled up with grandiose dreams and goals, most of which he actually had the courage to start.

To me, that is one of the greatest lessons a father can teach his son: Just have the courage to start and the dedication to finish when what you start when creating, or re-creating your own future.

Dad always had a burning desire to set his own intentions, and redefine his life (sometimes to a fault), regardless of what anyone thought or said. One day maybe I'll figure out if that "Gonzales desire" is rooted in courage, stubbornness, or stupidity. Hell, maybe the root tricates into all three of those elements. He was without a doubt the most stubborn, thick-headed, my-way-or-the-highway, myopic man I've ever met. I wonder how many of my friends reading this now understand that the apple never does fall far from the tree.

He never let the audacity of starting an adventure stop him from making memories with me. "Hey kid, we're going cross-country skiing," he said to me on one of our weekends together.

Oh my achin' ass, I thought.

He didn't care about the details; he just stuck with the macroplan of Napoleon Hill's advice: "Whatever the mind can conceive and believe it can achieve."

Or on another weekend

"Hey kid, we're going spruce hen hunting," he said to me. .

What the shit, over . . . I thought.

"Sounds great, Dad." I said.

*Sidenote: spruce hens are super gross to eat, especially when you bite into a shotgun pellet. It's okay though. It was never really about the spruce hens we hunted or the salmon we fished for. It was only about building dreams and making memories.

LESSON:

The wise are discreet in all things. I don't need to know how my dad figured things out, I just need to remember that he took the time to prepare himself for whatever he put his mind to. Be *prepared* as best as possible to figure it out along the way, and not just *ready.*

CHAPTER 31

OYE COMO VA, PAPA CHUCK

*T*he blood of Mexicano men is laced with passion. Passion for good food. Passion for women. Passion for our faith. Passion in the reverie of our own self-confidence and importance. And of course, passion for music.

Music artists of the 1970s and 1980s will never sound as good on CD or Apple Music as they did on my dad's record player. Just something about that crisp and vintage sound of memories when the needle dropped. Maybe it's not so much the sound of the music as it is how the memories make me feel. #OyeComoVa

"Oye Como Va" is translated into "listen how it goes," or "listen to the music." Don't just hear, but listen to and feel the music, not just the words. Envelope yourself in the lyrics, the rhythm, the instruments and understand what it means to you and why you enjoy it so much. I am guilty of

letting music touch my soul each day, to the point when it can bring me to tears of gratitude or tears of sadness. I'm so Mexican, sometimes.

I imagine this is also why researchers like David Hawkins, in his book Power Vs. Force, places a higher vibrational frequency value on Classic Rock than modern rock and roll. It's not necessarily the music, but the music and the memories that resonate higher for us Gen-Xers. Often times that energy gets the best of me.

When we "oye como va," or feel and allow the music to touch our soul, we feel a connection to the universe, to Spirit, and to our own hearts. Our hearts can be wicked, betraying us in a moment with its fickle, machismo flames fanned with musical accoutrements of the moment. Yes, our heart can turn on us and our loved ones in a moment, but we're also passionate about forgiveness and mercy. We're transparent about the brokenness of our heart, the longing for the woman who left, and how much better it would be to not go on in this life without her at our side. Combine a steady supply of alcohol to this moment and you have "un hombre con el corazón roto." A man with a broken heart.

Just as alcohol is a mood enhancer, music is also a mood enhancer. Dad loved his time listening to the blues, jazz, and classic rock, whatever matched his mood at the time, for whatever he was doing. Gardening, house repairs, car maintenance, fishing and camping, or watching a fire outside at his fire pit. Now, my cousins and I also listen to the same songs as our parents, to remind us of the time we spent with them, most of whom are all gone now. It's funny, I recently discovered my Uncle Dickie in SoCal had some of the same, not-so-well-known jazz albums that my father owned in Alaska. His daughters and I now listen to the same music as our fathers, I'd venture to say at the same moments, with the same passion, in the same moods as our fathers did. History is repeating itself before our very eyes.

I'm sure people in each generation have songs that remind them of their parents. The kind of songs that can stop you in your tracks and take you back to a time of either joyfulness or pain. For me, "Spill The Wine" with Eric Burden and WAR takes me back to happy times with my dad. I asked him once why that was his favoritest song.

"Because man," he replied. It just reminds me of peace." I think he actually meant "p.i.e.c.e. . . . "

I can still hear him singing it loudly in his goofy, rockstar voice, sounding like a low-budget Dr. Hook.

Fats Domino, on the other hand makes me smile but also makes the friggin hair on my arms stand up, because that was one of my mom and dad's drinking albums, usually followed by a midnight game of angry-food-fight in the living room of the single-wide trailer. Booze and bullish energy (my mother and I are both Taurus), mixed with flying eggs, leaving shattered "eggspectations" and a mess I was to clean up the next morning (dad joke!).

Good or bad, we all have songs that play in a language only the memories of our heart can understand. Sometimes it's the hardened part of the heart that's flamed, and sometimes it's the softened part that's sparked.

Before a road trip for camping and fishing with my dad, I transferred the vinyl to cassette tape. That way we could oye como va conjuntos (together) and he'd be proud of me for learning some of his favorite songs and acquiring his taste in music too whenever we went fishing up north for kings or down south for reds. Bumpin' Santana, cruisin' to Fleetwood Mac, or rollin' to The Stones as we entered the campground with our fishing gear and his 99 bottles of beer.

A funny story about Fleetwood Mac; when I was little, my dad told me that Stevie Nicks sang all of the songs, even the ones where she sounded like a man. I always thought that was strange, but he thought her voice was amazing because it had such a wide range. As it turned out, Stevie Nicks didn't sing all the songs. I discovered about 15 years later, Lindsey Buckingham and Christy McVie (God rest her soul) sang vocals, also. I thought it was hilarious, but really, it's not that funny, is it? (That's another dad joke!)

I went up to Alaska to see my dad in 2019, and we listened to Fleetwood Mac on his record player. I told him something like how talented Linsdey Buckingham was as a guitarist and vocalist on the track "Big Love." Dad gave me a confused look, I think because he still thought Stevie Nicks sang all of the songs! I didn't have the heart to tell him otherwise.

Forty years later, I still think of him every time I listen to Fleetwood and Stevie Nicks. It's okay, Dad, you can go your own way! (dad joke #3!)

For me I'm sure the answers to life's greatest questions can be found in two things:

1. The Bible
2. Bob Dylan songs

We listened to a *lot* of Bob Dylan on our drives, so by the time I was about 12, I knew most of his songs on his greatest hits album by heart. I still can't figure out why it's called "Rainy Day Woman #12 & 35" and not "Everybody Must Get Stoned." It's a mystery I'm still trying to get to the bottom of, but the answer is still blowing in the wind. (#4)

Steven Jobs said you can discover so much about a person by the playlist on their iPod, because it is so personal. "A thousand songs in your pocket," he said. I prefer the thousand songs in my dad's vinyl collection though.

I think we can discover a treasured-history from the vinyl they kept organized on the floor next to their stereo. From Champion Jack Dupree to Sonny Terry and Brownie McGee, Herbie Mann to Tracy

Chapman, Dad always loved the peace and serenity his music had to offer him. I wish I could have turned on Luke Combs' version of Fast Car and just "oye como va" together with him near an Alaskan-sized fire in his front yard.

My sons and my daughters might be beyond my command, but my boys and I absolutely love going to record stores to find old, vintage pieces of art. My oldest son Gabriel just bought me Pearl Jam's *Ten* on vinyl last week, too, and my nine-year-old, Maxwell, always tells me his favorite song is "The Chain" by Fleetwood.

Hope you're proud, Dad, because you passed down your taste in music to your grandchildren, and the times, they are changin'! (#5)

LESSON:

The goal of a father isn't to have great kids; it's to have really fun, respectful, successful, grandkids who have great taste in music and understand that Bob Dylan's songs contain the answers to what blows in the wind. Music is a gift given to man after the Lord looked upon us with blessings. However, Lucifer was also the minister of music in heaven, which is why he tempted Johny with a fiddle of gold. So, "oye como va," and try to hear who it is trying to touch your heart and move your hand.

*As luck would have it, I now live outside of where the sun comes up on a sleepy little town, just up the road from China Grove.

Here is a link to one of the playlists I made for him.

https://music.apple.com/us/playlist/papa-chuck/
pl.u-RRbVo87sxqmApg

I'd love to hear a playlist you made for your dad.
Send me a link at info@thelastalaskanmexican.com

CHAPTER 32

THE EPIC ALASKAN HIGH SCHOOL WRESTLING PARTIES

*M*y stepmom is going to kill me for telling this story . . .

After my brief time at Holy Rosary Academy, I decided two years was enough for my religious education. I felt I had done well enough to try public high school again so after my second attempt at the eighth grade, followed by the ninth grade, I enrolled at Robert Service High School in Anchorage (Go Cougs!). And what better way is there to meet new friends than joining team sports? As the son of a former Staff Seargeant in the Air Force, I also had the benefit of making friends with the young G.I.s, Dad worked with and supervised. Let me explain the connection between these two groups of friends.

My dad had a soft spot in his heart for G.I.s. He was a G.I. himself for four years, which is how he wound up in Greenland and eventually,

Alaska (BTW, G.I. stands for government issued). After his tour, he spent 30 years in the civil service, where he had the pleasure of working as a civilian, yelling at enlisted servicemen, getting saluted, and not having to wear a uniform. It was the best of both worlds.

He knew most of the G.I.s in his unit were away from their families in the lower-48, so he always invited these young soldiers over to our house on weekends for dinner, or to watch football, or sometimes to go fishing. Most of them seemed to be either from the South or from the East Coast, so Alaska was quite the culture shock for them, especially a Civil Service, Mexican Staff Sergeant in Alaska.

When I was a teenager living with my dad, some of these GIs were closer to my age than they were my dad's, so I got along with them pretty well. One thing I remember is how well young G.I.s on base took care of their cars. Every time I went on Elmendorf, it seemed guys were always shining their cars in the parking lot of every barracks we drove past.[*]

When I went to Anchorage for my dad's funeral in 2022, I went to Gold's Gym for a quick workout. A couple of GIs were in there, and can you guess what they were talking about? Yep, their new cars. It was October in Alaska, and this guy just bought a muscle car to drive on the snow and ice. Some things never change.

Two guys in particular from New York were among my favorite servicemen: John and Rich. These guys kept their cars spit-shined clean, ate pickled pigs' feet out of the jar (I think Wilma bought pigs' feet just for them), sprinkled mozzarella cheese sticks with garlic and washed it down with vinegar. Oh, and before they went anywhere, they were sure to bathe in cheap cologne. I could smell them a mile away.

In 1992, my dad and Wilma flew outside to get married in Las Vegas, and my dad thought it would be a good idea for John to watch the house and me while they were away. Of course, John would make sure that we stayed in line, didn't cause any trouble, didn't drink any alcohol in the basement at Dad's bar, and didn't have any friends over. Boy, was John in for a surprise.

John ended up becoming one of our favorite people to hang out with—mostly because he had a car, didn't have many other friends to occupy his time with in Anchorage, and wasn't too much older than we were. So, we'd have him drive us around town in exchange for getting his own private tour of south-central Alaska. It was a win-win, so I decided to take advantage of the relationship and throw a wild, high school party while the cats were away. After all, John was a friend of ours now, and he was a New Yorker, so there was no way he'd rat us out.

The captain of the Service High wrestling team found out that my parents were out of state, so he voluntold me that we'd have the annual, *epic* wrestling party at my house. I was too scared to tell this guy no, and I needed to make some new friends anyway. The next thing I knew, that weekend about 50 kids filled my dad's house—then, suddenly, that exploded to at least a hundred kids and their parked cars filled our entire neighborhood. They were in the backyard, upstairs, downstairs, in the trees, on the roof,—they were everywhere. All night it was a steady stream of teenagers coming into our house.

John was working his night job as a security guard and then came to the house to check up on me.

"Charles! *What the—! You said it would be just a couple of friends!*"

"It's okay, man. We'll get it cleaned up by the time they get home. Don't worry."

"If Mr. Gonzales finds out, he's going to kill me!"

"Dude, it will be okay." I assured him. And I couldn't believe he called my dad Mr. Gonzales. I'd never heard that before.

John was 100 percent *terrified* of what would happen to him if my dad ever found out we turned his house into a Las Vegas spring break event. To help ease his mind, when the party ended at 3AM, we started cleaning everything to a 'T.' I mean, we spit-shined the entire place like a G.I. spit shines his car. Until now, (as Wilma is sure to read this), my parents never discovered our epic wresting bash party. I even took photos of the living room *before* the party to make sure I put all of her heirlooms and knickknacks back in place properly. If there was one person who knew exactly where anything and everything was placed in our house, it was Wilma.

Another interesting story happened that night.

I had one, particularly ultra-crazy friend who had no shortage of bad ideas that would eventually become a few great stories. We've all had at least one of those crazy friends at some point in our lives, right?

My friend, a self-proclaimed genius, decided that it would be a good idea to light a road flare *inside* my dad's car as we drove it around town. Mind you, I definitely was *not* supposed to be driving his car around town either.

My hands clinched around the steering wheel, I looked over and started yelling at him, *"What the hell are you doing?"* The flare was dripping on the passenger car seat and burning holes through the upholstery! "Throw it out the window you dumbass! Throw it out now!" I can laugh about it now, but there was no laughing back in '92.

Continuing my tantrum, I kept yelling at him, "What the shit are we going to do now? First we have a party, now you burned up my dad's seat! He's going to kill me!" In an attempt to calm my nerves, he very calmly looks as me and said, "Chuck, don't worry, I'll take care of it."

"What the hell do you mean you'll take care of this? How exactly are you going to take care of it? My dad will be home in two days and there's no way we'll be able to 'take care of it' by then!"

"Chuck, just drive to my house. I'll take care of it."

We drove to his house and walked upstairs to his bedroom where he showed me a stack of hundred-dollar bills under his mattress. I had *no* idea why a teenager had a stack of one-hundred- dollar bills, but I didn't ask any questions, because my parents were getting home in two days.

We drove the truck back home and parked it in the garage to figure out how to remove the burnt passenger seat. Turns out it's not that difficult. We loaded it in a buddy's car then drove across town to a local upholstery shop, where I had a real honest conversation with the clerk at the front desk.

"Hey man, we F'd up, big time. We burned some holes in my dad's car seat with a road flare, in a truck we weren't supposed to be driving, and we need to get this fixed ASAP. We got cash. Can you help us?"

The guy just looked at us, dropped his head and started laughing!. "Don't worry guys, I got you." Ha! The angels *were* watching out for us!

By some miracle, they actually had the cloth material to match my dad's 1984 Ram Charger, and they repaired the seat for us in less than a day. Pretty sure that good-ole'-boy behind the counter felt sorry for us and put in a little O.T. to get it fixed for us on time.

On the same afternoon my parents arrived back in Anchorage, we picked up the seat, but we *still* had to reinstall it ourselves! We were down to about one hour before they landed at the airport. (My stepmom is going to kill me when she reads this).

We rushed home to install the seat, and *voila!* We finished with about 30 minutes before my parents arrived back home.

There was just one problem . . . the seat was completely brand new! This was a '84 Ram Charger that had over 200,000 miles on it, and now there was a frickin', brand new upholstered passenger seat! *Son of a mother!*

I looked at my friends and yelled, "Shit! What are we going to do? How do we make this thing look 10 years old? Wait, I got it!"

I found a broom and dustpan and swept up as much dirt and dust as I could from the garage floor. I held the dustpan over the newly upholstered seat, then gently and strategically began to sprinkle the dirt and dust and rub it in. I even sprinkled a few ashes from the cigarette tray on it to give it that slightly pre-owned look and smell. It wasn't enough, though, so I took some old coffee grounds from the coffee pot and gave it a few "strategy-stains." My friends and I were all pretty proud of ourselves and high-fived each other. We did it! LOL!

Dad and Wilma arrive home a few minutes later and were none the wiser. I did get an ass-chewing, though, because I left a few dishes in the sink, a dirty stove, and I didn't take out the trash. It could have been worse.

Currently, I'm writing this story *before* I fly to Alaska for my dad's funeral service. When I see Wilma in a few weeks, I have a feeling I'm going to get another ass-chewing.

Please pray for me, everyone.

UPDATE:

*As it turned out, I did not in fact get an ass-chewing from Wilma when I flew back to Alaska for the funeral service. Instead, she shared a few words of wisdom with me that I will pass along to you:

"Don't worry, Charles. It's called karma. You'll see."

It took me a few second to comprehend the possible consequences of the kind of karma since I have with three boys of my own. "Ah shit! That's way worse, Wilma!"

LESSONS:

1. Don't ignore the words of elders, because there is nothing under the sun they haven't seen.
2. Don't let crazy friends play with road flares inside of a vehicle.
3. The best stocking stuffers for a young GI are a container of leather cleaning wipes, car air fresheners, and a bottle of cheap cologne.
4. Karma is real. When I owned my personal training studio, I asked a client and friend from India to tell me his beliefs about karma. In his thick Indian accent, he paused, turned to me and said, "Chuck, all that karma means is that one day, you'll be doing the burpees, and I'll be doing the counting."

CHAPTER 33

THE PRODIGAL SON WHO SOLD HIS FATHER'S TRUCK: PART 1

*C*ar salesman: *"I'll give you $3,000 for it."*
     Me: *"Alright. It's yours."*

Most of my family and very old friends have been waiting a long time for me to tell this story. Uuuuuugggggggghhhhhh . . .

I recently discovered that my father attended an all-boys school, after getting caught stealing a car with his brother Gilbert and joy-riding around Los Angeles. Well, as I've said before, that apple definitely didn't roll too far from the tree.

I wasn't even sure if I would tell this story because it's the result of my dad and I being really stubborn, dumb, with *zero* patience, spending two years apart from each other without any communication. Two full years. Also, this story is more about me instead of my father, and I didn't want it to take away from the spirit of this book, which is supposed to be centered around him.

Then, I realized it is part of *our* story, and it's a fairly important period in *our* relationship. Therefore, it's an important piece of our history to share between my father and I in this book, and for anyone who's struggled in a relationship with their own father. For other readers who have ever chosen stubbornness instead of forgiveness, or anger instead of healing, this story that will forever be a thorn in my shoe has just one final lesson: Forgiveness.

My father and I didn't always get along. During a period in my life as a young man, I became blessed with the wisdom of King Solomon, the knowledge of all the prophets, and the understanding of kings of old. As with most teenagers, these blessings came to me when I was around 15-16 years old.

Like most teenage boys and their dads, we fought like cats and dogs a lot of the time I lived with him. I didn't even move in with him until I was 14, and it was a new experience for him to live with a teenager full-time and for me to live with my father.

He'd never lived with any of his children as they grew older, and I had never lived full-time with a father-figure before (not to my memory, anyway). It took some time for us to get used to the new dynamic, and I didn't just fight with him, but I fought tooth and nail with my stepmom, Wilma, also.

It wasn't exactly easy for me—pretty much an only child growing up with two adults who worked the swing shift. That left me with *a lot* of time to make some bad choices and coast through high school with a D, sometimes F, average. Call Steve-O, because I was a gigantic jackass.

Occasionally, Dad let me drive his Dodge Ram Charger around town, telling me that the car was insured and not to worry. I'm sure you can tell where this story is leading . . .

Anchorage has a notorious stretch of road in midtown that's called "The Strip." On Friday and Saturday nights, it's packed with teenagers in their parents' vehicles (station wagons, bugs, and other grocery-getters). Now, I'm sure it's overrun with electric cars and vaping teenager. I'd bet dollars-to-doughnuts there's still 22-year-old G.I.s cruisin' The Strip tryna' pick up high school senior cheerleaders in their spit-shined cars.

One Friday night, I drove my dad's Ram Charger down to The Strip to do what teenage boys do. Crusin through mid-town with the windows down and music blaring, we were having a great time trying to flirt with any girl we met on Friday night. A few friends of mine and I were sitting in that 1984, sky-blue precursor to the full-size SUV, when to the left of us, we heard a car full of teenagers yelling, *"Chuck! Chuck!"*

I turned and looked, excited to see a carload of my friends flagging me down. In utter excitement, I slammed the truck in reverse to back up and drive over to see them.

Without looking in my rearview mirror first, "BOOM!"

I looked over and saw my friends' shocked faces. I had *rammed* (no pun intended) into a little car that was stopped behind me. The owner of the car jumped out, completely pissed off, kicked the side of the truck and started yelling at me. I couldn't blame her.

Then she grabbed her neck in pain and started walking around her vehicle.

I had completely destroyed her car. Her front end was demolished. The radiator leaked fluid, the headlight was crushed—it was just a mess. My night was ruined. Hell, I thought my life was ruined.

The police came to write a report and give me my first citation.

"Can I see your proof of insurance, please?" The officer said.

"Yea, let me get it. My dad told me he has insurance. It's his car."

I searched the glove box high and low. It was nowhere to be found. "I'm sorry officer, I can't find it."

"Okay son, just be sure to find it and take it to the judge. Otherwise, you're going to have your license suspended."

I didn't know what I was going to do. Our truck was fine, just a dent in the bumper. But what was I going to do about getting this lady's car fixed? How was I going to tell my dad?

The next morning, my dad walked into the kitchen where I was waiting. Does everyone's father appear ten feet tall and bullet proof when you're about to get in trouble, or just mine?

"Dad, I have something I need to tell you. I got in a wreck last night." Then the interrogation began.

"Ah shit, kid. What the hell happened? How bad? What kind of wreck? Was it your fault? Did you get her information, and did the police show up?"

After fielding as many questions as I could while lowering my head in shame, I took him down to the garage and showed him the back of the truck. "I'm sorry, Dad. It was my mistake. I told the officer that you had insurance, but I couldn't find the proof and didn't know what to do."

With a serious and regretful look on his face, Dad stood there looking at the garage floor and said, "Kid, I don't have insurance."

This is when my world started spinning rapidly. I thought, *what the actual shit is happening and where in the hell am I right now . . . I'm so confused.*

"Dad, what does that mean? What should I do?"

"Listen kid, *you're* going to have to figure it out. I'm putting this car in your name because I don't want anything to do with it, and I'm not going to pay for or be liable for your screw-up, you go it?. You figure it out."

I was sick to my stomach, and I had no idea what I was going to do. I had no money, no job, no car, I was graduating high school in a few weeks and now I had to pay to repair a vehicle some how.

A few weeks later I received a *wonderful* letter from the DMV that my license was being suspended for operating an uninsured motor vehicle, and they would only reinstate it once I had high-risk, SR-22 insurance for three years, and proof that I was reimbursing the other party, since I was at fault.

This was the start of a very bad period for my father, Wilma, and me. I had to figure this out on my own, and now I didn't have a license. We were constantly at each other's throats day and night, and all I wanted to do was stay in my room and not interact with either of them. I had graduated high school and started working at a department store for that summer of '93 until I was headed to college that fall.

Then, I received another little piece of joy in the mail from the lady I hit, stating that I owed her $5,000 in car damages and medical bills. Things were going from bad to worse for me.

Eventually, Dad told me I needed to move out of the house. He told me to "pack up my shit and put it in the garage," then if I wanted to keep living there, I could politely ask, and as long as I agreed to follow all of his rules, I *might* be able to bring all my belongings back inside.

"I'm not staying here. I'll be out by Saturday." I said. I was already too damn stubborn to go along with his game.

"Good. Be sure to pack every damn piece of your shit and take it with you." I can still remember the anger on his face as he stood there in my bedroom doorway yelling at me.

All week long, I slowly boxed up all my things and took them to the garage. Imagine: A teenager's boxes of childhood toys, a couple of trophies, cassette tapes, and a few pairs of jeans, boxed up with no plan for the future. Sure, I was stubborn, but that was just hiding how scared I really was.

What would I do? Where would I stay? I needed a plan and all I had were the clothes in my boxes. But I did have a Ram Charger that was in my name. So I started concocting a plan I'm not very proud of.

A few days earlier, I had made a spare key to the truck. Friday night came, and I waited for my dad and stepmom to fall asleep after he tied one on when he got home from working the swing shift on the Air Force base. I wonder how many other Gen X parents did the same thing after working their shifts.

After they both went to bed and entered REM sleep a few hours later, I snuck downstairs into the garage around three in the morning. I watched lots of ninja movies in the '80s and '90s, so I knew exactly how to tiptoe and be invisible if I wanted. I opened both truck doors and the back hatch to the Ram Charger, then slowly and quietly loaded what little I had into the vehicle.

I was stealthy, I was quiet, and I was still terrified. I knew what I was doing would separate my dad and me—possibly forever. But I just couldn't take living there anymore, or his drinking, and his totalitarian, machismo attitude any longer. Worse yet, even a few friends and family members had encouraged me to leave the house with his truck (legally, my truck).

"I'll show him!" I justified internally to myself. "Maybe he'll finally learn to stop being such a selfish a-hole!" I said anything to convince myself that I was making the right decision, regardless of the consequences.

Now, the moment of truth. The truck was packed, and I had to push the button to open the garage door and pray to God it wouldn't wake them up. That 30 seconds it took for the garage door to open felt like I was looking down the barrel of a gun, and I only had a few more seconds to live. But . . . they never woke up.

I pushed the truck down the slope of the driveway and coasted into the cu-de-sac, where I'd be far enough away from the house to start it without the noise of the engine waking them up. Some genius I was. I left the doors and rear hatch open when I was loading the truck for a few hours, and all of the interior lights were on. Guess what that did to the battery?

Dead. Dead. Dead! I heard the dreadful "dry-clicks-from-hell," as I tried to turn it over in the middle of the road. Click-click-click-click-click. "Oh shit, this is it. I am completely done for." I said to myself. Then the sun started to come up over the mountain range in Anchorage.

You know what made the whole situation *way, way* better? We were in the middle of an ice storm in Anchorage. There was half-an-inch of ice all over the roads. You can't make this stuff up!

I knew I had to push the truck down the little hill so I could coast down and at least get out of sight, but I was just slipping on the ice every time I tried to push that damn thing!

Finally, I found *one* little patch of asphalt that I could get my toes onto to give me some leverage, then I pushed. *Voila!* The truck started coasting, I hopped in and was able to get a jump from a car driving by. Alaskans are pretty helpful to each other.

I still didn't know what I was going to do. I called my brother Raymond (not that one, the other one) and asked to stay with him for a few days. As any concerned brother or family member should have done, he called my dad and made arrangements for all of us to meet and for me to give him the truck back.

This was the brother who fought day and night with *my* father, his stepdad, when my parents were living in that damn trailer. Raymond knew the mistakes he had made with my father, and he didn't want me to make the same ones. Ray humbled himself enough to call my father on my behalf after they had not spoken in years. At the end of the day, Ray was just trying to take care of his little brother by trying to broker a peace deal between my dad and me.

But as soon as I got wind of this deal, I hightailed it out of there because there was no way I was going back to that house. There I was, with no plan, no place to live. Just a pathetic, homeless, handsome, humble, lost, little shithead teenager (7 of 8 of those are true).

All I could think of was to sell the vehicle and get my butt to college on student loans from the state. So that's what I did.

I sold the truck to a used car salesman whose business was on my dad's commute to work. Dad saw the truck each time he drove to work for a few weeks until it was sold. I didn't intend to be that spiteful; it was just the first dealership that offered me $3,000.

A few months later, I enrolled in college at the University of Alaska, Fairbanks only because I followed a smart and beautiful girl up there. I couch-surfed with friends for the summers, became a commercial fisherman, and didn't talk to my dad for two years— a two-year silence. Eventually I regretted that decision and missed him every day.

Then, over Memorial Day Weekend of 1995, his mother and his brother both died. . . .

CHAPTER 34

THE PRODIGAL SON AND A TWO-YEAR SILENCE: PART II

"But the father ordered his servants, 'Quickly bring the finest robe and put it on him; put a ring on his finger and sandals on his feet."
—Luke 15:22

These years we lived together were very hard on my father, my stepmother, and me. So many times I remember him saying, "Kids are to be seen and not heard." That made communication pretty difficult between us, but it made that two-year silence feel justified, somehow.

He really believed kids were just expected to be fixtures in the home, with no value or input to offer. Dad wasn't always the fun, old, wise, and loving grandfather he became in his golden years. Like most Baby Boomer fathers, it was either his way or the highway, as he reminded me and Wilma, every damn day.

Why? Their generation didn't have it easy growing up, and they had to learn how to turn wrenches and get their hands dirty from their own fathers who fought to win one of the most important wars in the history of the world. Since they didn't have it easy growing up, they sure as hell weren't going to make it easy for their own kids.

Nope, it was his way or the highway, and rightly so. He worked hard to get from the streets of L.A. as a kid, into the upper-middle class neighborhood of South Anchorage off Oceanside Drive, and he wasn't about to let some snot-nosed, "entitled" teenager get off scot-free. He made damn sure I knew how to read a tape measure, organize a socket set by size, how to change out the spark plugs, change my own oil, shoot a rifle, make my own bullets, and gut a salmon. All the things a boy should know how to do.

He never taught me too much about patience, listening, communication, or empathy, and it's taken me a lifetime to scratch the surface of those values. He and I had to discover humility and patience for ourselves—and a two-year silence was just the lesson we both needed to help discover them.

His mother gave him a hard time about not speaking to me. She told him to pull up his damn big-boy pants and get over it, because he was just the same when he was my age.

"Charlie," his mother said. "You were the same damn way when you were a kid. Remember when I shipped your ass to that all-boys home because you and Gilbert stole that car and drove it around Los Angeles? Charles is doing the same damn thing, and you're not doing anything about it. So what, he took your truck and sold it; you did worse than that! Now track him down, both of you make up with each other, and put everything behind you."

Dad never contacted me. He was too stubborn, and once again, the apple didn't roll far from the orchard.

Fastforward two years later. On Memorial Day weekend of 1995, Dad's mother and his brother Gilbert were very sick and admitted into a hospital in Los Angeles. Grandma' had diabetes and as a result had her left leg removed below the knee. She always said, "I call it my pegleg, mijo." I wasn't too close with my grandma' or Uncle Gilbert but nonetheless, they were still family and we all knew both of them would be gone soon. I knew my father still would have been too stubborn to take my phone call, so I reached out to my stepmother, Wilma. I told her I wanted to connect with my father again, because life is just too short, and I couldn't take the distance and separation any longer.

I think everyone knew Grandma and Uncle Gilbert were not coming home this time. She had family at her side and said, "If I go, I'm taking Gilbert with me."

I imagine as she lay there, she must have wished for my father and me to reconnect again.

Gilbert died on a Friday and Grandma died the following Monday. I guess Gilbert thought the same thing she did: "If I go, I'm taking Mom with me." When I heard the news, I broke down and knew I needed my dad.

After speaking with Wilma, he agreed to meet me at his house. When I arrived, we stood there in his driveway staring at each other, after two years of being angry and not speaking. We were still angry, but we were both broken, because he just lost his mother and his brother

"It's okay, kid. I know your grandma would have wanted this, too. I'm sorry, son."

I wept in front of him for the first time that day. Crying and humiliated in the arms of my father, we began our journey of reconciliation.

Ever since that day in 1995, my father and I became like best friends. I looked forward to calling him on Sunday nights to talk about the Rams or the Dodgers and hearing his roaring laughter, followed by his smoker's choking cough. It's always what I looked forward to on any given Sunday. And I have never forgotten the lessons of humility and forgiveness a father and a son discovered on that day.

Now I'm blessed with three young men of my own and one of them is following in my footsteps. Maybe that's a second book for another day.

LESSON:

Like rain in a desert, forgiveness has to be poured over others and ourselves during the hardest times of our lives. I can only assume that this story is why I am now naively forgiving to a fault, because those are two years that I'll never get back with my father. Forgiveness is never easy, but what value is there in that which is easy? Nothing. The right time is always now for forgiveness.

CHAPTER 35

"CHARLES, FIRST OF ALL . . ."

1. *"Don't let your kids join the military"* and
2. *"Don't let your boys watch the Oscars."*

One thing about my dad....

He was always worried about two things when it came to my three boys:

1. They would join the military, and,

2. They would grow up to be gay.

After I had my three princes, those were pretty much the only two things he worried about, and he never let me forget it.

Dad was in the Air Force, and it provided him with a great career for 35 years. But he knew that he was one of the lucky ones and that many young men of his generation wouldn't come back home if they joined the military.

He was in the Air Force during the tail end of Vietnam, while his brother, Gilbert "El Guapo" was in the Army. The eldest brother,

King Richard was also in the Army. Gilbert was never the same after he came back from the Army (see story #27), and I'm sure that's why my father worried about his grandsons joining the service. He just couldn't bear that kind of heartache again after watching his own brother come back so broken by the military. Dad was protective and didn't even want me to join the military for the same reason. I nearly joined the Air Force as an officer when I graduated college in 1997.

For as long as I can remember, my dad always discouraged the military as a career choice for me and my boys. He was so concerned we were going into some kind of a global conflict with Russia, Iran, Iraq, China, or North Korea. He stayed current on global conflicts because it made him feel informed with an intelligent opinion that people should listen to. He was thrilled when I started having kids and would say, "Good! That means they won't draft you if we go to war!"

That was the farthest thing from my mind when I became a father.

Now, I can't tell you why my dad was so worried about my boys being gay. Maybe it was just something from that generation, combined with his machismo-Mexican culture, which created his aversion to gays.

I mean, he had nine brothers and sisters, and my mother has seven brothers and sisters, all in southern California. You *know* there are a few gays in our family . . . not that there's anything wrong with that! LOL! #IYKYK

There are just so few people in Alaska that there isn't a lot of cultural or lifestyle diversity. Back then, the per capita of these reported, cultural demographics were below the mean of the lower-48, so Dad didn't have a lot of exposure to contrasting—or maybe in his mind, deviant—values, which were contrary to Catholicism (which he didn't even practice, but certainly preached) and his beliefs about family. He never went to Mass, lived in sin unmarried to women, had children out of wedlock, and didn't think we were supposed to eat pork like the Israelites in Leviticus. Don't throw stones, Pops.

Years ago I called him on a Sunday night during the Oscars. He said, "Kid, don't let your boys watch that stuff!"

"Uh, why not?" I asked.

"Because! They're going to grow up to be gay! You can't let them watch all that horseshit!"

"OMG, Dad. They're not going to become gay just by watching the Oscars. I mean, it's not like I'm letting them play soccer."

(I'm joking! I'm kidding! I'm joking! Oh man, I'm going to hear it now.)

"Well, what would you do if they did grow up gay?" He asked. That pushed the pause button in my universe.

"What did he just ask me?" I thought. "Did my own father just ask if I would still love my kids any differently if they were gay?" The listening ears of my intuition perked up and turned inwards, "Okay, Charles," my inner voice said to me. "Turn this into a teaching moment for your father."

"Dad, seriously . . . I'd love them just the same, and I'd respect their decision. It's their decision anyway, not mine. I mean, that's why you're in Alaska, 25-miles from nowhere, right? It's always your decision and you've asked us to respect that about you, which we do. So, we have to respect the decision anyone in our family makes about their lifestyle. Why are we even talking about this?"

"Because, kid! That's a sin! You can't be living a lifestyle like that!"

"Shit fire, Leroy!" I yelled back. "You remember how long you lived with Wilma for before you married her? Seven damn years, Pop! It's the same damn sin! And how many years did you live with mom *after* I was born before you married her?"

Maybe he just thought it was a "compound" sin; to be gay and live together might be in his mind, double-the-sin. To be fair, the Catholic church doesn't line item gender when cohabitating outside of marriage. It's not a double-whammy, or a buy-one-get-one. It's all the same sin as far as we're concerned. But, Dad didn't see it that way. He was honestly surprised to hear me say that I would continue to love my boys, my own flesh and blood, even if they were gay. "No Dad, you're not going to pray the gay away if any of them come out of the closet. Sorry, life doesn't work that way. Family doesn't work that way either."

When we finished our conversation, I couldn't help but think that for once I may actually taught him something. For once, maybe he actually listened to me. Perhaps that was a lesson he needed to hear from me about what unconditional love really is, and that real love isn't based on my conditions, my rules or my beliefs, but comes from a place that isn't rooted in a list of check-marked boxes for someone's approval, but rather from a place that has no restrictions or boundaries. Because it transcends time and space, love has the ability to skip gleefully back in history or forward into the future, if we allow it to. Love is the ultimate time and space pirate.

It's been quite a few years, but I only remember meeting about four gay people in Alaska. I'm sure I met more, but at the time I didn't notice or even care. It's wasn't exactly the most queer-friendly state back then, and to me, my father and my state seemed so damned closed-minded that I knew I could not create the kind of future I wanted for my family. This is why I left in 2000 to live outside in the lower-48.

At the end of the day, I don't regret leaving to seek new experiences, understanding, and wisdom. I wouldn't be the man I am writing this book if I had not left, and maybe I would have never discovered what love truly is and how it ought to be shown to others, especially to those in our own family. I can only hope perhaps I taught my father two important lessons in life:

LESSONS:

1. Military service is a great honor, and any child who is brave enough to join should have the full support of his or her parents.
2. The Oscars aren't going to make anyone gay . . . ever. But regardless, if your kids want to watch the Oscars or play soccer, a good parent should always support them. Not that there's anything wrong with that!

CHAPTER 36

FROM BOTTOM SHELF TO BOUJEE COFFEE

*O*ne thing about my dad, he never bought the good stuff.

I'm at the age where instant, black coffee is good enough for me. Maybe it's the mortgage and bills, or maybe it's just the cringe I get when paying $3.50 to a barista for a grande. These days, just give me a tablespoon of instant coffee in a cup of hot water. My God . . . I *am* turning into my father!

I drank Folgers coffee until I was about 30 years old, because that's all my dad bought, and let's face it, as much as I tried not to be, parts of me are a products of my childhood environment. For most of my adult life to that point, I searched for that two-pound, red container perched high on a lower-middle shelf on the coffee aisle in the grocery store. I didn't know anything was better than Folgers, because it was the only coffee I'd ever had, and I I didn't know what I didn't know. As far as I could tell, picking out coffee was like picking out cold and flu medicine: They're all basically the same, right?

Then in 2002, I moved to Portland, Oregon—second place for coffee-snob capital of America (first place goes to Seattle). As soon as those roasted arabica coffee beans hit my taste buds, I knew there would always be a non-negotiable budget for the grande, morning starter fluid (not too different than his budget for whiskey, beer, and cigarettes). I immediately thought about how disappointed my dad would be for my wasting my money on that "bullcheet coffee," as he would say. Or, *"Piss on that horseshit, mister!"* I also thought he might take away my man-card whenI told him I started paying to have the oil changed in my truck. He understood, though, because sometimes saving time is more valuable than saving money.

In the spring of 2022, a few months before Dad passed away, I walked into a Starbucks and noticed a little green thermos for sale on their display shelf.

I'll be damned, I thought. It was a miniature Stanley coffee thermos, just like he used to bring fishing with us—the old one with the little silver cup that screws onto the top, which all working men of his generation kept forever and carried with them to work and to the campground. I was instantly transported back to the banks of the Willow, where nothing could hurt us or make us afraid. I had to buy it.

I walked to the counter to pay for my order, and the barista commented on how nice the thermos was.

"Yea, it's just like my dad's. He would bring it with him when we went fishing together in Alaska," I said.

She paused for a minute, put her hands on her cheeks, and tried to keep from crying. The image of her emotion unexpectedly touched my own heart, then, I felt the tears begin to well-up in my own eyes too. We both just looked at each other for a brief moment and smiled, both trying to hold back our tears. I think we wanted to hug each other and just say "Thank you" and "Everything will be okay." I left the store feeling a little more light-hearted, albeit a bit embarrassed too.

My father had not even died yet, and the damn memories of this guy were still making me cry in public.

The barista and I went our separate ways, and I don't think I've spoken of this moment since then. Even now, writing about this still tears me up. Who knew coffee and the eternal, green Stanley thermos could make a grown-ass man so emotional? In all honesty, now that I'm in my late 40s, instant coffee is good enough for me, and now I understand why Dad saved his money and didn't always buy the good stuff.

Little had I known just a few months later, another lady behind the counter, this time at an ice cream shop in San Antonio, would bring me to tears too by unexpectedly brining memories of my father to the surface. I wonder if it was the same lady. Maybe the same angel, serving their customers through coffee and ice cream.

LESSONS:

1. Sometimes the memories are sweeter than honey.
2. Those who drink will be thirsty for more.

CHAPTER 37

THE DAY THE
ROCKY ROAD DIED

"You know Dad, there might be a God in heaven after all."
— Gabriel Carlos Gonzales

Unable to stand, I sat alone in silence inside my home on the staircase. His sister, my Aunt Vivian called, this time with no laughter laced her voice. I only heard the heartbreak as soon as she said my name; "Charles..." I could already feel something was very, very wrong. "Charles, your dad died." The sound of her voice is something I'll always remember. Her tone, and the inflection of heartache breaking each word will live forever within me.

She called to tell me that her favorite brother, "Charlie," as the family called him, had passed away in his sleep peacefully on his couch, in front of his windows overlooking the Alaskan wilderness. Wrapped up in his blanket, lying on his couch with a half-empty bottle of beer, and a half-pack of Terryton cigarettes next to him on the coffee table. He went out just like he wanted, and he was one of the lucky ones.

I knew this phone call was inevitable, I just hoped it wouldn't come so soon and that he'd have just a couple more of those Alaskan fishing summers left in him. I've never lost a father before, he was the only one I ever had so I didn't know what to think or feel when I heard he wasn't here with me anymore. I defaulted to my Catholic grief and the thoughts of what I had not done, then shifted into the selfishness of regret and of the things I had done. The anxiety I created instantly started building within the center of my mind and chest, and the mounting pressure and pain steadily grew silently within me. The only sounds were the random creaks throughout my home, and the wind blowing outside.

All I could think about was whom I could text, what I needed to do, the plane tickets, and all the things that didn't really matter when I should have just honored and paid attention to the moment. I couldn't believe I was going through this alone, and the creaks upstairs were reminding me that all of this was in fact very real.

Oddly, I didn't cry, and instead I just thought about how my life had recently unfolded, justifying my purchase of a new home in Texas instead of taking the boys out of school early, before summer break, and flying to Alaska to see their grandfather. He had always refused to get on another plane to come and see his family in the lower 48.

Creak, creak, creak. . . .

With my head in my hands for what seemed like an eternity, the reality set in slowly that for the first time ever, I was on earth without my father. Yes, this was actually happening to me.

Creak, creak, creak. . . .

What the hell? I thought. *Is someone home? Did I forget someone was here?*

I quickly dismissed the passing thought, unable to concentrate on anything at the moment.

I paced around the living room not knowing what to do. Not knowing who to call on Sundays. Not knowing who to make laugh with old fishing and snow machining stories. Not knowing who to call on my drive home from work. It was all so easy, so automated and "conveniently habitual," when he was here.

I knew that I had to tell my three sons first. I needed to be with and hold them as soon as I could.

I picked Gabriel up from work a few hours later so I could tell him myself. He climbed into my truck, just like he had for the last 19 years, and we sat there quietly, listening to Bob Dylan's "Like A Rolling Stone." It was one of my dad's favorites.

"Gabriel, this was one of your grandpa's favorite songs."

Gabriel, named after the archangel 'Gabriel' in the Old Testament (the patron saint of communication), felt the energy of the moment, and rather than reacting, he calmly gathered his own wisdom in his silence, then after a moment replied "What do you mean was?" Gabriel is as empathetic as they come.

I bit my lip, kept driving onward, and for the first time since I heard the news, I began to weep over my father. I think it was the second time Gabriel had ever seen me cry.

"My dad died today, Gabriel."

I think Gabriel knew it was coming. He was all heart and didn't say too much. He let it sink in for a moment just as I did when Aunt Vivian called me. His wisdom is much calmer than my wisdom. That's my boy.

We drove randomly around North San Antonio in my truck. I named my truck "Jackson," because my dad always used to slap me playfully on the back when I was little and yell out, *"solid back, Jackson!"* I still have no idea where he got that from.

We pulled into the parking lot of a 31 flavors ice cream shop, because just as my dad used to take me for ice cream after swimming Sundays, I needed an ice cream moment with Gabriel.

We walked inside, and I looked at my go-to: Mint chocolate chip. But I also saw Rocky Road, which my dad's favorite kind of ice cream. I *never* liked that flavor, ever. Marshmallows just don't belong in ice cream.

But I needed Rocky Road that day. A single scoop of chocolaty, marshmallow ice cream on a sugar cone to drip down my hand under the hot San Antonio sun.

"Wait a second; can I get the Rocky Road instead, please?" I asked.

The tears started to well-up again. The lady helping me behind the counter could tell something was emotional for me, and she was super sweet. She just looked at me with a warm heart, a cool head, and a soft smile. I could feel her compassion, and that helped calm me a bit.

"It was my dad's favorite," I said to her. She smiled with an empathy that can only come from a woman. That was the second woman behind a counter who nearly brought tears out of me with memories of my father. Maybe the same one, or the same angel who sold me the green thermos.

Gabe and I walked back outside in the 100-degree weather, ice cream melting down our hands and making a mess everywhere. It was the best ice cream cone I ever had, and for a moment, I felt as if I was walking in my father's shoes as I led my son back to the truck.

Then I looked at the car parked next to us . . .

Reading the energy of the moment, I stood still and staring at the car I said, "Hey Gabe, check out those plates."

They were Alaskan plates. Right here in San Antonio, at a random ice cream store, parked right next to my truck.

Gabe stood there quietly for a minute, contemplating, just my dad did.

He turned to me and said, "You know dad, there just might be a God in heaven."

The older Gabriel gets, the more he reminds me of his grandfather. I wonder what the silence of Kennicot mine in McCarthy would whisper to him.

Later that night, it occurred to me what the creaks must have been. For being so spiritual, I kicked myself for not being so observant. Thank you, Dad, for stopping by to check on me before you hopped on that heavenly low-rider, rollin' to streets of gold.

LESSON:

We *must* shed tears of sorrow and joy for those close to us who have passed away. We *need* to release mourning and grief for our loved ones—to open the faucet of our heartache and allow it to drain away before it robs us of our own strength.

If we allow it, bottled up grief won't just rob us of existing, but steals years of *living* away from our purpose. The ones we love are at rest, so let them be at peace. We do them no good, and we only harm ourselves when we hold on tightly to heartache and worry—and it will not add one more day to our lives.

Finally, recognize the importance of a cool head and a warm heart, and the need for ice cream when it's needed in the moment.

CHAPTER 38

THE REGRET OF ASSORTED CHOCOLATES

Hopefully, he's swimming in a river of caramel up there, and eating king salmon made of milk chocolate.

I've got a few regrets in life, just a few. It's valiant to post: "Live life with no regrets!" which looks really great as a tattoo but we all know it's not true.

Eventually, we'll let someone down by not finishing what we start, not doing what we say we're going to do, or not having the courage to start. In this case, I let myself down by not following through, and for me, that is *one* regret I do not give myself forgiveness or mercy from. I'm my own, loudest, harshest critic, and there can't be anyone worse than me at sending off things in the mail, especially bulky things that don't fit in a regular-sized mailbox. It's the whole process of finding a box, putting said object(s) in the box, tracking down the shipping address, putting the package in my truck, remembering that it's actually *in* the back seat of my truck, and remembering to drop it off at the overpriced shipping store. I've just never been very good at that whole process, which is why I live with the regret of assorted chocolates.

Living down here in the Lower 48, I can walk a mile down the road and get the best chocolate candy, birria tacos, or ice cream I've ever had. On the other hand, Dad had to drive 25 miles just to get a dozen eggs for $4.99 (um, that was back in 2018). In his small town of Wasilla, about 40 miles north of Anchorage, he couldn't get:

- A decent, damn Mexican tamale
- Ripe avocados
- Fresh oranges or fresh fruit
- A fresh bouquet of flowers for the love of his life
- Great men's clothing (fashion in Alaska is when your snowmacheen suit matches your snowmacheen).
- Or, great chocolate candy. My legal team tells me that I shouldn't use the name of the candy store, but it sound very similar to—Tee's Candy.

In of October of 2021, I bought a box of 'Tee's Candies' to send to him. He had a major sweet tooth his whole life, and I'm sure it grew even sweeter in Alaska, knowing he just couldn't get it anytime he wanted. Absence makes the sweet tooth grow sweeter, as they say (I'm not talking about just sugar either).

But what I really purchased was a good intention, a novelty, an ambitious attempt at offering my father a reprieve from the uninspired sweets of the north. But, that novel intention just wasn't important enough for me to send off in the mail. And that "intention" sat in the back of my car for seven months.

I'll be sure to stop and mail it tomorrow! I thought.

"Okay, I'll send it when I take lunch," I said.

"I'm working out of town; I'll send them when I get back." I tried to convince myself.

I don't know why I never had the initiative to send it off. Why? What was my *power of why* for not putting it in the mail to him?

- I was too focused on my own priorities
- I thought I had all the time in the world, and I was greedy with my own time.
- I was proud that I was the only one sending him his favorite chocolates, and I didn't need to hurry, because he'd get them when I was ready to send them.
- I didn't want to deal with the hassle of traffic, lines of people, and the millennial customer service rep, who would drive me up a wall.
- Shipping was so expensive. Besides, I needed that money to buy more protein powder.
- He already enough chocolate that he stockpiled along side of his whiskey, beer, and cigarettes, and didn't need another excuse to keep him on the couch, in front of his TV and massive view of the Alaskan wilderness.
- I was just too lazy

I never sent it off. I was too busy making excuses.

As it turned out, a girl I was dating said, "Charles, we'll buy your dad another box of chocolates. In the meantime, we're eating this one because I need chocolate *now!*" (She was a little hangry at the time.) After sampling away one-by-one, I never bought him another box.

Then, he died on Sept 20th, 2022.

That's my regret. That's just *one* of my regrets in life. Imagine how I felt, knowing I wasn't just procrastinating, but I was being lazy, painfully prideful of my own importance and naive about how much time I thought I had left with him. How much time do any of us have with those we hold closest to our heart? The answer is always unknown.

I can't help but think of him each time I drive past "Tee's Candy" store, and I can still see that box in my back seat. After seven months in a car, it was just stale chocolate at that point. Served us right eating stale chocolate after not having the discipline to send it off. I got my own 'just desserts,' as it were, for procrastinating too long.

I hope there's a heavenly chocolate fountain and river up there with little, chocolate salmon swimming upstream, Dad. Because, if you're not up there, it's just going to be a bunch of super-hot melted chocolate and burnt s'mores down there. I'm kidding! Lol!

LESSON:

As I open my mouth in prayer, asking pardon for my own pride and laziness, all I can do is look for the wisdom around those candies; the silver lining around the cloud. One day I hope any wisdom I find will be absorbed by my own three princes, as is the hope of any father.

CHAPTER 39

BURYING MY FATHER INTO ALASKA

"Beneath those birch and spruce trees on the banks of the Willow, no one and nothing could make us afraid, ever."

— The Mouth Of The Willow

Micah 4:4

For as long as I can remember, my father wanted to be cremated with his ashes scattered in the ocean. Death wasn't anything I ever liked talking about, but a few years ago, I needed to have a very Catholic conversation with him about what the Church teaches.

"Dad, there needs to be a final resting place. You can't have a final resting place if your ashes are spread all over hell and back."

"I'll make that decision for myself, Kid," he said. Classic Gonzales. Damned stubborn, machismo Mexican.

Sometime in the last few years before 2022, he had told Wilma that he didn't want a big funeral service and that he just wanted to be buried in the ground, on the Elmendorf Air Force Base, in Anchorage where he retired. I was pretty surprised when she told me that they were burying his ashes in the Alaskan ground instead of the Pacific Ocean. Dare I say that maybe, just maybe I got through to him . . . once. GD he could be ornery and stubborn, cantankerous old sourdough.

About 20 of us gathered for his funeral. His ashes were in a small, black box. Not an urn, just a box, and I'm sure that's how he wanted it. Nothing fancy or expensive, just a little black, cardboard box.

I couldn't understand how someone who seemed as big as the Alaskan Mountain Range could fit in such a small compartment. I wonder what the alcohol and nicotine of those ashes were. It *had* to be over .02%, because I *know* he tied one on the night before he died. Dad got his final DUI on September 20th, 2022: Death Under the Influence. I wonder how much time he's serving for it in purgatory.

Dad's service was conducted with excellence. It was truly incredible to see such young men and women perform their duties with such intention, empathy, care, focus, and excellence for the family members.

As we stood in front of his headstone and a hole in the ground just big enough for his box, I watched a young construction worker thrust his shovel into a mound of dirt in a wheelbarrow to cover my dad with.

My red flags when up and once again my listening ears turned inward. Standing in front of me was a young man about to pour the very ground over my father that nourished us and fed our souls. I couldn't watch someone else bury my father. This was something I needed to do myself.

I stepped forward and said, "Sir, excuse me, excuse me. . . ."

"Chuck, what are you doing?" My cousin Nicole (Uncle Richard's daughter) whispered as she stood next to me. I'm sure everyone else there was thinking the same thing she was: "What's that jackass doing now?"

"I'd like to do that, please. I'd like to bury him."

He didn't know what to do. He looked at the curator, she nodded her head, and he handed me the shovel. I wasn't about to let some random dude backfill my father when I, a Gonzales, was standing right there. *Gimme that damn shovel. I was born for this moment.*

I stepped up to grab the shovel, then I looked at the same mountain range as I had a thousand times before. Beneath those snowcapped tops, I was getting ready to bury my father to rest at their feet, forever.

Shovel after shovel, I slowly poured the same ground over him that he loved with all of his heart. It was same ground we stood on around fires so many summer and winter nights before. The same ground we fished on all those summers ago. Now, he'll become that same ground.

I offered the honors to my stepmother, but she couldn't do it, which I understood. I offered the shovel to anyone in the crowd of 20 who came to pay their respects. They had a right to say their goodbyes, too.

One-by-one, his friends and family came to bury one of their favorite people, who led an amazing life, in an extraordinary place, in the largest city in America, within the biggest state, on the strongest nation, of the most powerful plant in the entire galaxy: Alaska, The Last Frontier.

I even brought home some of that same Alaskan dirt we buried him with.

Staff Sergeant Gonzales was placed in the ground on Ft. Richardson/ JBER, but damn it, I should have put a flask of whiskey and a pack of Tareytons cigarettes in there with him. Sorry Dad, but you had enough while you were with us, anyway.

At least he has a great view here on Earth from his final resting place in that ground—and an even greater one from above.

I love you, Dad. Love you too, Wilma.

LESSON:

One day, if we are lucky, those who loved us the most, those we stood together with, will pour over us the very ground we once stood on with them. We would be so lucky if that were our final blessing.

CHAPTER 40

I'M STILL PISSED

One thing about me . . . I'm still pissed at my dad for dying.

I don't know how long kids like me are supposed to be pissed for when one of their parents dies, but I'm still pissed. If you're reading this and have lost a parent, were you pissed at them for dying? How long am I going to feel like this? Are you still angry? I get the sadness part of losing a parent, but I don't think I expected to feel this angry at him, and for this long too. Here it is almost two years later after he passed and I still feel the heat in the center of my chest becoming hotter when I think about all the things I thought he had left to do.

I don't believe I've passed through all the stages of grief: 1) Denial; 2) Anger; 3) Bargaining; 4) Depression, and; 5) Acceptance. I think I'm just stuck on anger, and I imagine that many men default to anger, then sit there, marinating in their own defecation.

He was supposed to answer my damn phone call on Sunday and tell me about his weekend of fixing the RV, the four-wheelers, and getting the snow machines ready for the winter. How *dare* he die, leaving Wilma so much to do on her own! That selfish self-destructing, machismo-Mexicano should have known better than lie around the house all damn day, drinking and smoking and he *knew* he should have taken better care of himself!

"What in the hell did I expect?" I ask myself. "Here's guy who abandoned his two children and family in Los Angeles and started a new life 2500 miles away from them. He never thought of anyone else which is exactly why he made such a fool of himself each time he started drinking. He never cared about anything other than himself and his 'whiskey, beer, cigarettes,' while forgetting about his entire family. There is no amount of excuse on this planet for him being so damn selfish and lazy. And God only knows why I was born to an alcoholic father who didn't give a shit about anyone."

Sometimes I just have to step back from the picture of my own emotions hanging on the wall because I'm looking at it too closely. As I readjust and look at it from a distance, I can see it's crooked—unlevel. I take a deep breath and say to myself, "Whoa, Charles. Whoa. Calm down and remember isn't your plan, this isn't even your story, and you're not in control. Heavenly Father, change me, and bless him, please. All he wanted was to live his own life, and he wanted YOU, Charles to create your own happiness too. You're just here along for a temporary ride until your own Father calls you home. So, calm down and flow, Charles. Don't Force. Just flow. Take a breath, take a moment, and look at the picture again. Now it's level."

As you can see, my anger is obviously a protective mechanism for me. But as the saying goes, "being angry at an alcoholic means drinking your own poison and hoping the other person dies." I can't stay angry forever, I know this. Sometimes I just need a chapter in the book of my life to let out a little frustration. Thanks for listening and brining me back down to Earth. A little self love and grace can go a long way, and more importantly, can drop your blood pressure a few points too.

He was only 76, but he gave up on life, living out his last few years on a couch, watching TV—albeit with a great view of the great Alaskan outdoors from his living room, and with a woman he loved, who also loved him in return simply for who he was.

He lived all of the life he ever wanted. He was content with what he accomplished, the home he built, the career made in the Air Force, and he thought there was nothing more he needed to do. There was plenty I wanted him to do though, but I wanted it much more than he wanted it for himself.

I wanted him to watch his grandsons play football. He never saw any of their games.

I wanted to take him to the best sushi houses in town, and then taste the flavors of an Indian restaurant for the first time.

I wanted him to see my gym that I built to start a career—and to show him it wasn't just a hobby.

I thought we'd be able to drive to Seattle and see an NFL game, or watch even watch the MLS Portland Timbers play the Sounders with the Timbers Army thumping in the background.

I wanted to push him in his wheelchair along the River Walk in San Antonio when I moved to Texas, and stuff ourselves with the world's best BBQ brisket, then watch a music festival in Gonzales, TX, just east of San Antone.

But I have to reflect on my own intentions as a child and realize all the "I's" in what I wrote. As I re-read this I can feel the selfishness in the everything "I" wanted. No one can want something for anyone else more than they can want it for themselves. What did he want? "Whiskey, beer, cigarettes," as he often told me. This is a guy who bought $2000 in cigarettes before the Alaskan governor signed a bill that put an $0.11 tax on each cigarette. He just wanted to be happy and for him, that didn't include BBQ, the River Walk, football games or concerts. He discovered his own happiness in the home he built in Knik, AK, with a woman he was married to for over 35 years. It's funny how they know what's best for us when we're growing up, and how *we* think we know what's best for them when they're growing down.

My happiness was to have him buy my stepdaughter's Girl Scout cookies, donate to my boys' football fundraisers, and create memories with his grandchildren. But his happiness was a freezer full of cigarettes, and a fridge full of homemade menudo, and cheap beer. #Priorities

"Fat, dumb, and happy!" as he always said when I called on Sunday and asked him how he was doing. "My way or the highway," he'd say. The most stubborn man I ever knew, and that's saying a lot because my mother and I are both Taurus. The apple doesn't fall too far from the tree, but my tree of stubbornness lives in the shade of his. I think my anger has outgrown his though.

I stood next to his sister-in-law at the funeral. Shoulder to shoulder, we stared at his headstone in silence together, both shaking our heads and coming to terms that Carlos was no longer with us. The man who could fix anything, the one to call when your dishwasher stopped working or a breaker needed replaced—we'd have to figure out those things on our own now. How are we ever going to do it all ourselves?

I looked at her and said, "I'm pissed at him for dying, Aunt Betty."

I could hear the tears of sadness pouring from her heart as she turned to me and said, "We all are, Charles. We all are." Her heart cried drops of blood for my father, mine rained drops of fire. I don't think I'll ever not be pissed at him for dying, but then again, maybe there is a value in the anger. I just haven't discovered what it is yet.

LESSON:

I'm instructed to get rid of all bitterness, rage, and anger, and to be kind and compassionate, forgiving. Maybe one day when I grow out of my youth, the Almighty will give me the grace of such forgiveness. For now, I'm just hoping He'll just let me stay pissed for a little while longer.

*BTW, Dad was a Libra.

CHAPTER 41

GET OFF YOUR 'BUT!'

One thing about my dad, we used to talk most every Sunday night.

I used to call him nearly every Sunday since he'd probably be watching tape-delayed football in the late afternoon, and maybe 60 *Minutes* at night. When I was little and it was his weekend with me, I used to love watching football and the old 60-Minutes on Sunday with him. I truly enjoyed watching Morley Safer, Ed Bradly, Mike Wallace, and my favorite, Andy Rooney as we wrapped up our Sunday night eating dinner in the living room on the coffee table. It was such a treat to watch Mike Wallace rip into anyone he interviewed. They were all men of action, men of The Greatest Generation who changed the course of history by NOT procrastinating.

Rooney was by far my favorite though. I just felt there was something special and nostalgic about watching a WWII veteran tell his short stories about old typewriters, or what a real car horn should sound like when you honk it at someone.

"I try to look nice. I comb my hair, I tie my tie, I put on a jacket, but I draw the line when it comes to trimming my eyebrows. You work with what you got." —Andy Rooney

But on September 20th, 2022, Dad's sister called me to deliver the news that he passed away, and guess what I **DID NOT** do two days before that Sunday? I **DIDN'T** call my dad. I thought I'd call him later, in another day, maybe in two days. "I have enough time and I can always call him tomorrow." That's one decision I'll regret for a long, long time.

I'm too busy, but I'll call him tomorrow.

I have to workout, but I'll call him tomorrow.

I have to go grocery shopping, but I'll call him when I get home.

I need to get just a little more work done, but I'll call him afterward.

A few years ago, one of my favorite motivational speakers and life-changers, Sean Stephensen coined this term and wrote his book, "Get Off Your But." It's simply about recognizing when you're stuck and not making any progress, and some simple things you can do to—get off your but. I was stuck on my "but" for some reason that weekend.

I'm sure Dad is telling me right now not to be so hard on myself. I'm sure he's looking down, telling me to forgive myself. Maybe one day, but I doubt I fully will. I'm Catholic, Alaskan, Taurus, and Latino so I'll probably hold on to this guilt (and anger) for a while longer.

I find myself getting "stuck on my but" the older that I get. I mean, how long did I let those chocolates sit in the back of my car for? I'm not sure why I'm getting stuck on my but more often, but it's something Dad would definitely not approve of. There's no power in procrastination and it only leads to mounting pressure, anxiety, and self-doubt. These are values my father did not teach me and are only products of my own comfort.

The older I get, the more I understand that my own father spent years staying off his "but." To him, there was no problem too big for him to handle, because everything was "figureoutable." He was too damn stubborn to give up and refused to give in to the temptation of "but."

"But it's too hard!"

"But it's too expensive!"

"But I don't know how!"

"But it's too hot!"

"But it's too cold!"

"But it's too far!"

"But it's too dark!"

"But I can't get fresh avocados, tomatoes, onions, cilantro, jalapenos to make guacamole! Okay, I'll give him that one.)

"But it's too bright!" (The Alaskan midnight sun)

"But I'm too tired!"

"But I can always call him after *60-Minutes* next Sunday."

In my previous story, I questioned the value of anger in my heart. What I've come to understand, nearly two years after my father passed away is that anger, my anger, is a reminder of time, or rather the *lack* of time each of us has here with one another. Time moves so fast for us these days that none of us should make room for the "buts" that keep us from living. Rather, the "buts" that move us forward are the only "buts" we should make room for.

"But I don't have the time to put this off any longer."

"But I may never have this opportunity again."

"But this is bigger than I am, and I need to follow through."

"But the time is *perfect* to get this done right now!"

"But I know I can do this!"

"But this is too important to not share with the world."

And finally, my favorite "but:" "But I only have a certain amount of beats."

The architect who designed and helped build my father's house asked me one day why I was jumping rope and exercising. "Charles, why are you jumping rope? You're just wasting your beats."

"Um, What? What in the conspiracy-theory-hell are you talking about now?" I replied.

"Listen Charles, The Good Lord only gave us a certain amount of heartbeats in this lifetime and you're just wasting them on exercise. Slow down man, don't burn through your beats too quickly."

Yeah, sure I could argue with him, but at the end of the day, he's not wrong.

Don't waste your beats waiting for the perfect moment. NOW is always the perfect time to make all of your beats count.

LESSON:

If there's a lesson here, it's this:

DON'T. LISTEN. TO. YOUR. BUT. It will keep you from that which matters most. I have lost so many damned friends and family lately, there's just not enough time for buts in this world anymore. So, don't waste your beats.

*I actually wrote Andy Rooney a handwritten letter around 1996, asking him not to retire yet because his stories were too important, and my generation needed to hear them. Whether he knew it or not, he helped preserve a piece of American history, and even brought sons closer to their fathers through laughter in living rooms across the country. Maybe Mr. Rooney has an influence on my own writings too. As it turned out, he didn't retire that year after all.

Maybe one day my kids will understand why I loved watching 60-Minutes.

CHAPTER 42

MY FATHER'S FINAL LESSON: "SON, YOU'VE GOT TO LEARN TO FORGIVE."

*D*ad, *you have no idea how hard this lesson still is for me to learn.*

Sitting in my home office in San Antonio, I glanced over and found an large, manila envelope that my stepmom, Wilma had sent to me 13 years earlier. I had briefly looked through what she sent me in 2009, but I'm sure I was too busy with the kids, changing diapers, and running my old gym to focus on what was inside. I thought it was just some genealogy records of my family she had put together for me.

I'll go through it tomorrow, I had thought.

That "tomorrow" took 13 years, and in 2022, I finally looked through everything that was inside of the envelope. In the very back of the pile of geneology letters was the judgment/decree from my parents' divorce in 1983. I'd never seen their divorce decree before, and as a result, I now know what vertigo must feel like. It literally shook me to the core and sparked an anger I didn't even know lived inside of me .

My mother divorced my father, claiming that he was an abusive husband to her and an abusive father to me. She accused him of being a violent and unfaithful alcoholic and asked that he not have any visitation rights to see me without attending counseling and an alcohol treatment plan. She also asked for full custody, $400 a month in child support, and that I would be *only* allowed to see him every other weekend until I was 18; he was to have *no* contact with me in between his visitation rights.

My heart became a bass drum and my liquid, Taurus-anger started dripping from my soul and burned through the center of my chest. All I could think of was how much time I had missed with my father, because of my mother's vindictive nature. Powered by her vanity and pride, she managed to convince that damn judge that she was Mary Poppins and my father was Ike Turner. Part of me hopes there's a special place in hell for that judge.

How many fishing trips did I miss with my father?

How many football games *didn't* we get to watch together on Sundays?

How many segments of Andy Rooney were we robbed of?

How many stories by the campfire did I never hear?

That's when I called my dad.

He answered the phone. "Gonzales, *what is it?"* He asked.

"Yo, Pops, what it be like!" I'd reply.

"Hey Dad, so check this out. You know what I just found after 13 years? I found the divorce decree that Wilma sent me from yours and moms divorce. I could wring that GD judge's neck!"

It took a few seconds for it to sink in for him. At that point, everything took a few seconds to sink in.

"Wait, what are you talking about, kid?"

"The divorce decree for your and moms marriage. I'm just now reading everything the judge said."

"What the shit, over! Thirteen years? What in the hell took you so damn long?" He said, with a deep laugh in his throat, followed by the smoker's cough for about a minute.

"Well, *I've been a little busy!* Raised kids, got divorced, sold the house, and moved to Texas!" My father and I never really spoke with anger at each other. It was always with light-hearted frustration.

"I just read this judgment from the divorce, and that damn judge said you couldn't have visitation rights until you went into a treatment program? *What the shit! She was drunk every damn night and beat the shit out of me!*" I yelled.

My father's exact reply: "Kid, I don't even remember that, man. Why are you still so mad? That was such a long time ago. It's time for you to forgive, man, and you can't stay that mad for so damn long. You know it's not good for you. It's just time for you to forgive and forget, that's what I had to do. When was the last time you talked to your mom anyway?"

The great thing about being an alcoholic is that memories are easily forgotten. The bad thing about *not* being an alcoholic is that you remember most everything and those memories can fester like an untreated wound inside of you. And, it hurts really badly when the bandage is ripped off unexpectedly. I pray one day the Lord will weave patience and forgiveness into my bones.

"Dad, I haven't talked to her since Gabriel was born, and he's 19."

"Charles, that's just so sad, and I'm so sorry you haven't talked to her. I know how pissed you must be, but that's not going to help anything or anyone. I'm not pissed about it anymore, and you shouldn't be either. I know you wanted to try and protect your boys from her, but your boys are going to have to make up their own minds, and you can't protect them forever."

Pausing just a moment, he knew he was missing something, then broke out into his battle cry.

"Damnit, now I need a drink and a smoke. *Wilma!* Where are my damn cigarettes!"

The sound of her voice in the background is always unmistakable.

"Get your ass up and get your own damn cigarettes!" She'd yell back. I love that woman.

That was the last conversation I ever had with my dad. His sister, my dear Aunt Vivian, called me a few days later on September 20 to tell me that my father, her favorite brother, had passed away.

I'll always remember that final conversation and his final lesson to me—forgiveness.

SUMMARY

It's not until I started writing these short stories that I began to understand all the lessons and wisdom I chased after—all the business strategies and tactics and knowledge I searched for from coaches, masterminds, and leadership groups could all be found in my dad, within the most simple things and events in life. Beneath the cloud of cigarette smoke lay the lessons to life, love, faith, relationships, and even business:

1. Listen to your gut, it's never wrong.
2. It's okay to be afraid. Don't let it stop you though from reaching the banks of the Willow in Alaska.

3. A timid heart seeks few adventures, and remember the heart of courage.

4. Love your dad, because at the end of the day, love will be repaid to you.

5. Trust your father and His priests, lest you are overcome by the monsters of portable toilets.

6. Chase your dreams with the adventurous spirit of a child.

7. The Golden Rule: When you do good to others, that kindness will always be repaid to you.

8. If you don't gather anything when you're young, you wont gather anything when you're old.

9. Mind your language around your kids. Garbage in—garbage out.

10. Give to others, but also accept from others, especially when it's something that can bring you unfathomable joy.

11. Sacrifices must be made on the journey to enjoy the fruits that many will not taste. Put in the work, chase the goal, and the lessons will be found on the trail you take.

12. Moments create memories. Make those moments matter.

13. Your neighbors are not always what they seem, and what we observe is always skewed by our own ignorance and malevolence.

14. Sometimes, we don't have to look for the answers to life, we just need to listen to them instead.

15. No matter how much space separates us, we always have family somewhere, and we are never truly alone.

16. Sometimes the dream looks sexy, but on the journey, it's not always easy.

17. Everything is figureoutable.

18. Don't be afraid to start.

19. The cliff is high, the jump will be scary; don't be a baby, and laugh all the way down!
20. If you don't clean up your campsite, the bears will scavenge your space.
21. Be prepared, not just ready.
22. The unexpected consequence of any journey in service to God is discipline. And any discipline worth its weight should not come easy.
23. Have the courage to finish what is started.
24. Understand there is a time for anger and a time for forgiveness.
25. Sometimes, you just have to wash your hands and bow out gracefully, and that's okay. (I've never been good at either of those.)
26. Give yourself a little self-esteem, and at least try to remember the virtue of humility as often as possible.
27. Give a little grace to happy drunks. They're trying their best.
28. Don't always be so quick to discount the advice of medical professionals.
29. Lawd . . . I hope they know I'm just joking. Let's remember to never take ourselves so damn seriously
30. A good woman can add years to your life. I suppose the opposite is also true too.
31. It's the memories of black coffee which make it taste best to me.
32. It's never, NEVER healthy to stay bitter for so long. When enough is enough, release your anger, bitterness, frustrations and failure to Christ. Don't overthink. Life is too short to waste time on overthinking. Just start doing and figure out the details later.

33. Don't ignore the words of your elders. There is nothing under the sun they have not seen.

34. Like rain in a desert, forgiveness has to be poured over others.

35. Military service is a honor, and your kids won't become gay by watching the Oscars.

36. Shed tears of sorrow and joy for those close to us who have passed away. Don't be afraid to emote.

37. True wisdom is learning from our own failures and seeing the opportunity we are now smart enough to create.

38. One day, with a little luck, those we love the very most will watch us return to dust. This is a consequence of living a life worth telling a story about.

39. Growing up means leaving anger and bitterness behind us, not weighing us down and holding us back from our future.

40. Don't listen to your 'but.'

41. A good wife will add years to your life, and harmony among family is always pleasing to the eyes of the Almighty.

42. My final lesson is quite simple—forgive.

MY LETTER TO THE U.S. AIR FORCE FUNERAL SERVICE SQUAD

When my father died, Wilma arranged a small service at the Joint Base Elmendorf-Richardson (JBEAR) in Anchorage. It was a beautiful service that the ceremonial team conducted with excellence. Not many things are conducted with excellence these days, but the US Military is still one of the groups that strives to do things right. I just had to compliment them on such a well-organized event, conducted with care and empathy for all, especially my father's grieving widow.

"The work your team performed at my father's funeral on October 17th, 2023 was one of the most careful and thoughtful ceremonies I've ever witnessed. Each member of the team conducted himself or herself with purposeful excellence, and understood the importance of the role he or she played by honoring a former, American soldier.

"The curator, the chaplain, and each soldier put great care into the details of their position, and all extended a sense of warm compassion to each family member and friend in attendance, simply by choosing to be excellent. That is a value of the American military that cannot be found anywhere else on the planet, and I commend each of them and each of you for your service. A ceremony of calm heads, warm hearts, with conduct of excellence.

"I'm so proud of each of you, and I hope all of you are proud of yourselves for the things you probably don't realize sons and daughters of those buried see within you and are incredibly grateful for.

"I'm sure Carlos Gonzales was looking down on everyone with a very full heart. Hopefully, he wasn't looking up . . .

"God bless you all, and God bless the US Military.

"Charles Gonzales, a grateful son"

DENOUEMENT

I will always miss my father to the moon and back, and not a day goes by that I do not think about him. Ever since he died, I've entered into a different, much more lonely part of my life. Perhaps it's a right of passage for a man to lose his father, because it means now we have to figure everything out on our own, like he did. Now, everything must become "figureoutable" for me.

I will always regret not calling him the Sunday before he died, as I usually did each week. Some weeks are harder than others without him here, and I still find myself wanting to call him each Super Bowl, or simply to gloat about the incredible BBQ or Mexican food I get to have living in the Lower 48. It still makes me happy that the last Super Bowl he watched was with our team, the Los Angeles Rams, holding the Lombardi trophy high above their heads.

I'm still not a writer. I put a few stories on a few pages, but that doesn't make me a writer. I know my strengths and English literature, storytelling, and verbs are not my strengths. For me, dressing these stories up a bit to produce a few smiles and tears is my strength, if I have any at all. There is no shortage of edits or rewrites I could make for all 42 of these stories, and though I don't consider myself a great writer, I hope you enjoyed each of them.

The stories are true . . . enough, but not necessarily geographically or historically accurate. I tried to roughly estimate the timeline and list them in chronological order, but at the end of the day, it was just my best guess for some of them. And it's the story itself that's more important than when or where exactly they happened.

The lessons are for the reader to discover and not for me to prescribe. They are simply my interpretation of how the Wisdom of Ben Sira is trying to speak to me, and hopefully they resonate with you. I hope you find the knowledge and understanding in these lessons as I'm still trying to fully figure them out. #figureoutable.

What is most important for me when writing these stories is creating something that can bring a smile to your face, even a chuckle, because that's the memory of my father living on. And, if some of these stories make you shed a tear that glistens in the light of your iPad, Kindle, or wood-burning fireplace, well, that too is a memory of Papa Chuck coming to fruition, which I'm sure he's grateful for. If you listen closely in the distance right now, you can hear him yelling *"Orale! Gracias!"* for helping his son walk this earth without his father, The Last Alaskan Mexican.

GLOSSARY OF ALASKAN TERMS.

Alaskan Terms	Common Terms
Alaskan Native	Indigenous person born in Alaska.
Bug Dope	Mosquito repellant
Bunny Books	Insulated Rubber Boots
Chinook Wind	A warm wind
Combat Fishing	Shoulder-to-shoulder fishing along a river or a fishing hole.
Flat Top	A geologically-formed flat mountain in the Chugiak Mt. Range in Anchorage
Four-byin'	Off-roading in a truck or 4x4'n
Going Outside	Going to the Lower 48 or Hawaii.
Hooligans	A small, oily fish. Also, a group of young people searching for mischief.
Humpy	Spawned out red salmon
King	Chinook
McKinley	Mt. Denali (Den-Alley)
Mukluks	Traditional winter boots worn by some native Alaskan tribes.
Cheechako	New to Alaska; A greenhorn; A newbie. Inexperienced.
Sourdough	Old timer; Experienced; Seasoned outdoorsman.
Oosik	Walrus penis

Permafrost	Permanently frozen ground
PFD	Permanent Fund Dividend (They pay you to live there)
Pinks	Chum salmon (it's gross)
Reds	Sockey salmon
Run	A large school of salmon coming in from the ocean and swimming to the spawning grounds
Silvers	Coho Salmon
Sleeping Lady	A mountain visible to the west of Anchorage, which resembles a lady laying on her back
Snowmachine	Snowmobiles (to outsiders)
Solstice	Longest day of the year/shortest day of the year
Termination Dust	First dusting of snow on the mountain tops
The Bush	Rural Alaska, accessible only by boat, float plane, snowmachine, or dog sled (not to be confused with The Great Alaskan Bush Company).

www.ingramcontent.com/pod-product-compliance
Lightning Source LLC
Chambersburg PA
CBHW051417090426
42737CB00014B/2715